LAST TOUCH

Preparing for a Parent's Death

Marilyn R. Becker, M.S.W.

NEW HARBINGER PUBLICATIONS, INC.

Copyright © 1992 New Harbinger Publications, Inc.
5674 Shattuck Avenue
Oakland, CA 94609

Cover design by David Bullen Design
Cover photo by Taro Yamasaki

Library of Congress Catalog Card Number: 92-081726
ISBN 1-879237-34-2 Paperback
ISBN 1-879237-35-0 Hardcover

A somewhat different version of the introduction was published in the January 1988 issue of Ms. *magazine.*

First printing December 1992 5,000 copies

To my parents, Tess and Sid Becker, who knew when to hold me close and when to let me go.

I've only seen one old person die, and the energy of death and birth is exactly the same, a feeling of stillness in the air. The only difference is that as soon as the birth happens there is joy, and as soon as the death happens there is sorrow. But the actual transition—the energy—is really similar. With birth there is elation, with death there is grief.

—Rebecca, a midwife, quoted in *Hearts Open Wide: Midwives and Births*. Berkeley, CA: Wingbow Press, 1987.

Contents

Acknowledgments

So many people contributed to this book, in so many ways.

I would first like to thank those who shared their stories, Toby Benetti, Becky Donovan, Susan Eggly, Kathryn Haapala, Shea Howell, Fred Johnson, Rosa Naparstek, Catherine Perrin, Dan Ryan, John Scarfenkamp, Marcy Schlinger, Carol Yamasaki, Kim Yamasaki, Maria Langlois, and Susan Zaro.

I would also like to thank Joan Becker, Diane Borko, Amy Hanover, Jane Loubert, Mel Moore, and Emmaline Weidman for their sound information and helpful ideas; and all of my freinds, relatives, clients, and students for their varied contributions to this project.

Special thanks to Charlie Varon and Myra Levy, who helped me shape and edit this book; Barbara Quick, my editor at New Harbinger, who then polished the material and made it shine; and my agent, Bob Silverstein, who has a humorous and gentle approach, much needed and much appreciated.

Judy Sagarin-Steinglass showed her confidence in this project, even during the hardest times. And, finally, I want to thank my husband, Jack Kobliska, and our daughters, Rosey and Annie. They could be counted on as a constant source of love, friendship, and support.

Introduction

How My Mother and I Lived Through My Father's Dying

"Don't mention death to your father" was the note my mother passed me as he lay dying in a rented hospital bed in their living room in San Diego.

She was taking care of my father now that he could no longer take care of himself. She knew that during the course of his fatal illness I had often tried to talk with him about death. She also knew his reaction most of the time when confronted with his dying: God forbid.

So we did not mention it, my mother and I, as we cared for my father the last nine days of his life. He died October 24th at 5:00 a.m., in his own apartment, surrounded by what he knew and loved.

I prepared for this home death in much the same way I had prepared for childbirth. People joked that I was becoming a death expert. I, who had spent a lifetime hiding from the idea of death, barely able to say the word without spitting over my shoulder and knocking on wood.

But I knew I had two choices: I could deny what was going to happen and refuse to accept my father's death, although he would die anyway. Or I could try to help. If I wasn't afraid, we could talk and say good-bye.

I began by reading every book on death and dying I could find. I was fortunate to come across Stephen Levine's *Who Dies*, a book filled with the kind of stories I needed to hear. By the time I finished reading it, I felt that I would be able to handle the fear, and that I would know how to deal with the pain.

That is how my mother and I came to be sitting in the dining room eating dinner while, eight feet away, my father lay in his bed, dying. "Did you ever imagine you would be able to do this?" I asked my mother, who couldn't even visit cemeteries, so unwilling is she to look at anything that has to do with death. She laughed, "Never."

My father had been in that bed for six days, unable to move or talk and, for the past day, unable even to swallow food or water. Hospice, our main source of support, had told us that we could stop feeding him and giving him medication. His body was shutting down. Food would only make him more uncomfortable.

Eating, in the last six months, had been his favorite activity. He was always hungry. Now he could not swallow and he could not eat. This was hard on my mother and me, as we equated caring for him well with feeding him.

He lay in his bed, his right arm paralyzed and stiff, his fist clenched against his chest, so frozen up I could barely move his arm to change his pajamas. Purple blotches appeared everywhere on his dry, lifeless skin, like internal stains; his muscles were weak but tight from inactivity. No longer able to speak, he would bang his left fist down on the bed or shake the side bars when he wanted to communicate.

I was watching my father's skin, muscles, and bone literally fade away. For comfort, I'd consult *Who Dies*, and was reminded that a mere 500 years ago, people had as limited an understanding of the material world as we now have of the spiritual world. All people, *even the smart ones*, thought that the world was flat and you fell off at a certain point. People still fall off the earth, but now it's when they die. We see the body go but can't yet see what happens to the spirit.

Some friends have said, "Seeing your father become like a baby, having to wipe him, feed him, diaper him, hear him moan, must have taken its toll on you." And although this is true, it also helped me prepare for his death. It gave me something to do and allowed me to be of use instead of standing by helplessly.

The call from my father came early in April. "I've been in the hospital. I have brain cancer." Panic and despair were my initial reactions. I began to ask questions. What tests had been done? What was the prognosis? What were his choices for treatment? There were more calls back and forth, a search for hopeful information. Long-distance conversations with his oncologist, who, after giving me a lot of detail, said kindly, "I'm sorry."

On my first trip out to San Diego, my fear of flying was coupled with fear of my father's death. I could handle neither, but had to deal with both.

I arrived in the late afternoon and took a bus to my parents' apartment. My father was in the hospital with a high fever; my mother was with him. Unlike past visits, when they were both at the airport to greet me, I was on my own.

On the bus I sit next to a 70-year-old man from Yonkers, New York. He is drunk and telling jokes to the Mexican lady next to him, getting everyone, including our Irish bus driver, to laugh. The old man's friendliness and humor draw all of us on the bus together, and it is a rich moment. Suddenly, he falls back against his seat, his eyes roll back, and it looks like he has passed out. But soon it becomes clear that he has suffered a stroke: part of his body is paralyzed. Now his illness connects all of us. We go into action like a well-prepared team. I become the diagnostician; the bus driver pulls off the highway and phones 911. A young woman comes forward to help make the old man more comfortable; everyone has a suggestion to offer. Finally the ambulance comes and takes him away. The bus continues on its way, and I have begun my visit with a spontaneous, on-the-bus training program for medical emergencies. I wonder how many medical emergencies I will be facing with my own father.

I visit my father in the hospital. They have discovered that he has pneumonia. They can treat that. But he is despondent and negative, angry that he is ill. He starts to cry when I talk about his grandchildren, describing how they are doing. I realize that he fears he may never see them again.

When my father regains strength, we walk the halls of the hospital, my mother on one side, me on the other, his I.V. trailing behind. There are many others walking the halls with their I.V.'s and tubes of blood who look far worse than my father, but they smile hellos to those they pass. I want to look away so I will not see the wasted flesh, the pallid faces; so I will not become frightened. But I am moved, despite my fear, by their ability to live in new ways in this new place with all that apparatus. They will not be crushed by their illness.

I meet my father's doctor. He is a caring person who relates information to me respectfully; but I have five minutes, that's all. His beeper rings and he is off. He can't afford to give more time, emotionally or financially. He is working on the medical line, a technician doing his part. I long for someone who is a healer, but all I find are doctors.

That night in my parents' apartment, my mother and I sleep together. We awaken at dawn and begin to talk. We hold each other. Boundaries disappear. This is a moment that will shape the months ahead, a time when my mother and I draw closer, tending to my father's needs, weaving a much stronger connection than we have ever had before.

I return home to Michigan. My father begins radiation therapy. The treatment makes him tired and he loses all his hair. He complains, but is glad for a chance to shrink the tumors, and he regains some hope. He believes in his doctor.

I suggest to my father that he take Vitamin C, do creative visualization, exercise a lot, and change his diet. He barely listens, feeling safe only on the route outlined by his physician. I stop making suggestions.

In June my parents come to Michigan to visit. For the first time, my father looks old and frail. Just three months ago he was president of his condominium association, a vital, energetic, young 74-year-old. Now he walks slowly, rests a lot, and is very demanding. My mother waits on him. I wish he would act differently, but I know that he is very frightened and angry.

I take my parents on an excursion to Windsor, Canada. My father is having more difficulty walking; he is shuffling his left leg. I help him sit down on a park bench overlooking the river while my mother and I go shopping. I am almost afraid to leave him alone. The paper he is reading blows away and he cannot retrieve it.

A few days later, he has a seizure while sitting on my living room couch. We telephone the emergency medical service and they quickly respond. The shaking and convulsing lasted at most one minute, but it seemed like half an hour. My husband, Jack, is the only one who knows what to do, which is basically to keep my father from hurting himself. I rush between the first-aid book and my father.

I ride with him in the ambulance to the hospital. It is a very sad moment. This seizure means that the radiation hasn't worked.

My father only wants to go home to see his doctor. The emergency room staff give him anti-seizure medication and release him. They assume that he will fly home the next day.

By morning he can barely walk. While brushing his teeth in the bathroom he falls into the tub. Jack and I have to carry my father down the stairs. I call his doctor in San Diego as we are about to leave for the airport and he insists that my father cannot fly in his present condition. He must first get a CAT scan. I am upset but realize that the doctor is right.

My father is easily persuaded to stay, since it's his doctor's advice. My neighbor Kim puts us in touch with his personal physician, who is willing to admit my father to Henry Ford Hospital through a local emergency room.

Once again we are alone in an emergency room waiting to be seen. We had spent part of the previous night talking about dying. Finally death has been mentioned. He wants to be cremated and laughs when I tell him I had been planning to ask my husband to build a casket for him. There is some acceptance in his voice. He is not crying. We talk about my grandparents, who died in their late eighties. I tell him I had hoped he would be around another decade—he had always been so healthy. I wonder if it was easier for him because his parents were so much older. He thinks it was.

Now in the emergency room of Henry Ford, we continue our dialogue. Maybe there will be something else *these* doctors can do. His mind is still clear. He thinks up a list of hopeful signs. We talk about my mother. I assure him that she will be able to rely on me as she had on him.

Later that night, he is transferred to the hospital. He goes by ambulance while I follow in my car, crying the whole way there. I go up to his room and lie on the bed with him until the resident arrives.

The hospital gives him a battery of tests. He is seen by radiology, oncology, neurology. Finally, after all the results are analyzed, his doctor tells me there is nothing more that can be done. My father is going to die. I feel like I am going to faint while at the same time I am asking questions. I am holding on to the counter of the nurses' station. I ask where my father will be going. At first the doctor and the resident don't understand, but then they catch on that I mean where is my father going *after* he dies. The doctor says that they don't know the answer. They don't teach *that* in medical school. I ask to be the one to tell my father.

We go into his room—the doctor, the resident, and myself. I tell my father what they have told me. They ask him about life support if he should get sick, and he answers that he doesn't want it. Then he starts to cry.

We bring him home a week later. That first evening is a disaster, but it is also when my mother shows her true colors, bright and strong.

My father cannot walk, and we have not yet gotten a wheelchair. My husband is away, so she, with a bad hip, and I must carry him. We are able to get him into bed, but then he has to go to the bathroom. We struggle to get him there in time, then find ourselves stuck in my back bathroom, too small really for three adults to fit into, trying to lift him from the toilet to wipe him and turn him enough to get him out the door.

It is a frustrating moment. We could easily have started to cry. Instead our eyes meet and we are struck with the utter absurdity of the situation. We both start to laugh and cannot stop. That laughter must have released some extra energy. We are finally able to get him up, wiped, and out the door. He does not laugh with us, but he doesn't seem embarrassed or upset.

This is another moment that will shape the months ahead. At other, equally frustrating times, my mother the comic reappears.

In fact, a minute later, we are in another difficult situation. My father has to urinate; but before we can walk him back to the bathroom he loses control, urinating on himself, the floor, and the couch. "Oh well, it won't take long to clean it up," my mother says. How easily we adapt by turning these moments into commonplace occurrences that can be handled. Our language shapes our responses: "Oh well," instead of "Oh no."

That first evening turns out to be the hardest. Afterwards, we get all the equipment and help we need. We make the downstairs playroom into a sickroom. There is a bed from upstairs so my parents can continue to sleep together, a portable toilet, a bedpan, and his wheelchair in a room that is already filled with toys and books.

We also get home health care, a visiting nurse, and a physical therapist, who come twice a week. They are more like healers than doctors; they take the time to talk with all of us and never seem rushed.

My father improves to the point where he can stand on his own, then walk on his own. He approaches his physical therapy energetically. Each time Dee, the therapist, comes, they go for a walk. Soon he is able to walk around the block. Dee encourages him to take three long walks a day, but he is afraid to go by himself.

Chip, my husband's partner who is working next door, offers to accompany my father on walks. Three times a day for three weeks, Chip is there, slowly walking alongside my father. These walks are more than physical therapy for him. They are visible signs that he is getting better. He does not know or want to know that it is the medication that has improved his condition.

For another couple of weeks, things go well. We return the wheelchair. My father shuffles carefully around on his own. We start to relax. Then he falls bending down to retrieve a piece of candy and hurts his arm. I am away at a meeting in Detroit when my mother calls to ask me to come home. My father is very upset.

The next day, I take him to be seen by a doctor—another emergency room visit. But this time I have no resources to call on. I feel drained. I can't bear the sounds of the room, babies crying, people moaning. I can't bear to see all these people who look sick and injured. Whenever I can do so unobtrusively, I put my hands over my ears to shut everything out and close my eyes.

An x-ray reveals that my father has broken his wrist. He feels this to be a tremendous setback for him. After the doctors put his arm in a cast, I take him home. He is now depressed, and I feel unable to be cheerful. We are silent on the ride home.

But by the time his 75th birthday arrives a week later, my father has adjusted to his cast and regained his optimism. Now he blames all problems of balance on his heavy cast. We have a big party to celebrate his birthday. My cousin flies in from California. My father's closest friend, Mildred, whom he has known since he was 16, flies in from New York City. My whole community of friends comes out for the party. I worry that it will be a very sad evening and that I will cry, but it turns out to be a lot of fun. My mother plays the piano; Mildred, who is an actress, dances and sings, and we all join in. People stay very late. My father looks well and has a great time.

A few days later, my father decides that he wants to go home. I feel guilty: he and my mother have been at my house for two months; I am ready for them to leave. But I think he is planning to go home because he believes he is going to live, and I know that he is going to die.

I want him to know that he doesn't have to leave. We talk. I ask him where he would prefer to die. He tells me at home. But he also feels that he will enjoy himself more there while he is alive. And if he becomes ill again, he can return to Michigan. *If* he becomes ill again: he is still hoping for the best.

I drive my parents to the airport. My children remain at home. I know that I will be feeling very sad. I want time to cry. We arrive early. My father immediately has to get to the bathroom. He is too frail and shaky to be left on his own, so I go with him into the men's bathroom, standing in the doorway watching him in his stall. If he falls, I can quickly move to his aid.

We then walk slowly to the plane. My mother keeps up the conversation and we all hide in talk from the feelings we are having. Everyone knows how sad this moment is, but none of us wants to say it out loud. We act as if this were just another trip home.

I get permission to accompany my father onto the plane. I am planning to help him into his seat. But I am overcome with sadness. Any moment now I will begin to sob. I quickly say good-bye to the frail, shaky old man my father has become and rush off. As soon as my back is turned, I start to cry and continue crying through the airport terminal, into the car, and for most of the ride home. In fact, I miss the right exit and end up lost, going home the long way.

That evening our house feels empty. We all move around slowly, fixing dinner, cleaning up, not trying to get away from our feelings, just letting them out to wander about the house.

Two months go by. My father has adjusted well to being back home. My Uncle Henry stops by regularly to take him out for walks. Relatives visit and take him to dinner. My mother cooks enormous meals. Then he falls getting into a chair. Two days later, he falls in the bathroom. He panics. He is afraid to be left alone.

On the phone he cries. Finally he tells me, "If you want to see your father alive, you better come now." I decide to fly out immediately. I am spending too much energy trying to decide what to do. I can handle a few extra trips across the country, but I can't handle my father's dying without seeing him again.

I arrive in San Diego two days later. My father is propped up with pillows in his bed. When I enter the room he starts to cry. We embrace and hold each other close for a very long time. When we pull apart I see how bad he looks. His face is swollen and puffy. He cannot sit up without support. Our few minutes together have already tired him out. He asks for help to lie down and take a nap.

From that moment on he starts to let go. Each day for the next nine days he drifts further and further away. He has seen me again and knows that I will be there.

By nighttime the hospital bed arrives. Hospice has been contacted and they begin their enormously helpful support work. They provide all the equipment we need. They come to our house regularly. They teach me to change my father and his bed with him in it. They help us to know what to expect, giving me their infamous blue paper which lists the signs of dying.

But aside from the equipment and their physical and emotional support, the hospice people give us something even more important. They give off an aura: their presence provides a spirit of caring and acceptance that seeps into our pores and remains after the hospice staff leaves. They are calm and peaceful in the face of dying.

My mother and I try to copy their style. We make up a schedule and routine. My father needs 24-hour attention now, so she and I sleep in shifts.

The nights are definitely the hardest. My father wakes up a lot, needing help, and I am tired. But worst of all, when it grows dark, I start to feel afraid. As his death draws closer, I know that I don't want to be alone. And I want to spare my mother, who would have a difficult time watching my father in distress.

I call my cousin Joan in northern California and ask her to fly down that night. I am an only child, and she and I are very close. I know that my father will be dying soon. I have been checking that blue paper: I know by his symptoms that his body is preparing itself for death.

He has become incontinent. He sleeps most of the time. He often seems restless, pulling at his bed linen, constantly throwing off his covers. That was number seven on a list of ten. Number eight: "Your loved one will have decreased need for food and drink because the body will naturally begin to conserve energy which is expended on these tasks." Number nine: "You may notice a change in breathing patterns: breathing may become irregular for ten-to-thirty-second periods of no breathing."

My mother goes to bed at 7:00 p.m. My cousin arrives at 8:00. We embrace, then approach my father's bed. I can see her quickly move from discomfort and sadness to alertness.

My father has started exhibiting symptom number nine. It is very upsetting to hear. He gasps for breath, then sounds like he is choking, then doesn't breathe at all, then starts to gasp again. Over and over and over again. I call hospice. They explain that there is nothing we can do to help him. This is the Cheyne-Stokes syndrome. It could last 24 hours.

Joan and I sit close by my father's bed. We take turns brushing each other's hair and rubbing each other's back. We hold my father's hand and gently stroke his head. Wordlessly we find a common ground. To us it's as if my father were in labor. There is nothing we can do but keep him company. We stay next to him, occasionally lying down nearby to get some sleep.

Early in the morning, he stops gasping and choking. His breathing becomes almost imperceptible. Then he is still. At 5:00 a.m. as we stand next to him, he stops breathing. One breath and then no more. We wait and watch. No more breath. But even without breath he is still there. We stay by his side and watch him closely. After a while, I go into the bedroom and tell my mother. For the first time in six months, she starts to cry. I hold her and cry with her. "At least he wasn't in pain," she says.

Nervous, unsure of her reaction, she comes with me into the living room. Slowly she approaches my father's bed. She looks at him, then leans over and kisses his forehead to say good-bye. "I thought I'd be afraid seeing him this way, but I don't feel frightened," she says. "Let's keep him home a little while longer."

So we wait several hours before we call the mortuary. We brew a pot of hot steaming coffee which we have with almond croissants. The three of us sit at the dining room table having breakfast, waiting until we are ready to let my father go.

Hospice helps again. We are able to avoid police and coroners. By the time the mortuary men come, my father is gone from his body. My mother goes into the bedroom, but Joan and I watch as the two men take the body away. It seems as if they are taking away a pod, not a person. In fact, we giggle silently, for the two men wear dark sunglasses and look like seedy private detectives. We wonder to ourselves how it feels to do their job.

Afterwards we go downstairs to sit by the pool. The sun is shining and feels very hot. It is hard to understand this beautiful morning in terms of the last few hours we've shared. Both are real: the warm sun, watching my father die. We feel like proud veterans who have been given a chance to do something special. We are embarrassed about it, but admit that we feel like bragging. We swear then, we will only brag to each other.

Years have passed since my father's death. At times I want to renege on my acceptance. I don't want my father to be dead. But many of my friends are traveling the same territory. So at least I'm not alone.

My friend Chip composed a song for my father on the piano. He calls it "Sid's Minute." My husband and I took many of my father's clothes. We have his sweaters, jackets, and socks. We wear them a lot. I'm still collecting stories and reading—immersing myself in books about death. It's not that I'm stuck. I'm just not ready to move to a different place yet. My father is dead; he left me an invisible gift—a new connection to my ancestors' breath. And the experience of handling one of the hardest parts of life: death.

1

The Unfamiliar Terrain of Death and Dying

So Few Resources

After my father died, I couldn't stop talking about my experience. I wanted to share with others how we had lived through his dying. I began to realize that my friends and I needed a new tradition: we needed to trade stories of our parents' deaths as we had previously traded stories of our children's births.

It was not so long ago that birth was considered scary and secretive. There was little information available that explained what actually occurred. Men were left out of the experience entirely, told to stay outside in the waiting room. Only the doctors and nurses were prepared.

But I was fortunate to come of age during a special time, the sixties, and to be part of a generation that insisted on being involved in the decisions and events affecting our lives. We learned to discuss and explore subjects that other generations had kept closed, like sex, relationships, and childbirth.

Consequently, I was a veteran of childbirth education classes and the self-help movement. I was educated in the finest libraries and bookstores in the country; I developed a basic strategy to handle any new and potentially frightening situations. That strategy consisted of reading and talking—two things I do well.

The day after I found out I was pregnant, I was at the local bookstore sitting on a stool in front of the pregnancy and birth section, going through every book on the shelf. Nine months later I was an expert. When a fear arose, I comforted myself with statistics from one of the dozens of books I had. I learned the language, the details, the options of birth. And I developed a network of people I could call on with my questions and concerns: I surrounded myself with people who were involved in pregnancy and birth.

All the preparation and connection paid off. I had one very difficult birth, my first, which lasted three days, and one very easy birth, my second, which lasted three hours. I was prepared for both.

The day I learned of my father's terminal illness, I was back at the local bookstore, sitting on a stool in front of the three books they carried on death and dying. This time when I attempted to educate myself, I found limited resources. That is why I have written this book. *We need to be helped to prepare for death as well as we have been helped to prepare for birth.* We need more stories, more information, and more details so that we no longer feel frightened and ignorant.

I never saw myself as someone who was capable of dealing with death. When one of my high school acquaintances died of leukemia during my junior year, I quickly tried to forget it. I had little to do with my grandparents when they were dying. If anyone had told me that I would be enjoying a steaming cup of coffee and an almond croissant in my parents' dining room while my father's body lay a few feet away from me, I would not have believed them.

As a psychotherapist, I had always seen myself as part of a profession that could deal with taboo subjects like incest, suicide, and sex. But I had not been trained to help people with their repressed and often invisible anxiety around death. In my two years of graduate school training, I do not recall attending any lectures on the psychological implications of our individual and collective terror of death. In the 26 years I've been practicing, death continues to be a heavily avoided subject in the profession. Odd, since it's not as if some of us die and some of us don't, some of us will lose parents and some of us won't.

Clients don't often come in and say, "I'm scared of dying"; and, until recently, it certainly wasn't a subject I was going to bring up.

However, after my own experience with my father's illness and death, I found that I was better able to help my clients deal with their own parents' aging, sickness, and dying.

Everyone seems to start out in denial. I remember my own contact with that stage, when my father told me he had brain cancer. I wondered what I would do if my father died. And then it struck me: it wasn't *if*—it was *when*.

I recall a client who told me about a terrible fight she had with her mother, who was grossly overweight and had begun to develop serious health problems. "I don't know what I would do if my mother died." I gently pointed out that her mother was going to die, sometime. She seemed shocked by this knowledge. "I can't bear to think about that. She's always been there for me. What would I do without her?"

An editor friend, reading a draft of *Last Touch*, told me that the book would help a lot of people. Luckily, he was not one of them: "*My* parents aren't going to die," he said jokingly.

My friends and my clients were all eager to hear about my experience with my father's death. They couldn't stop asking questions. What was it like? How did you feel? What did you do? How did you prepare? What made it easier? What made it harder? Where did you find help? What does a natural death look like?

This book emerged from these conversations. At work, dinner parties, my college reunion, whenever people learned what I was writing about, they would volunteer their own stories, eager to have someone to talk to about their experiences.

The American Way of Death

Death is a part of life. However, in our society, death is hidden from most of us. Most of our choices that have to do with illness and death are made for us, not by us. But this has not always been so. One woman I interviewed was six when her grandfather died at home. She vividly remembers viewing his body, laid out in the parlor; it all seemed quite ordinary to her.

In traditional societies, and indeed for nearly all of human history, death has been an accepted, natural, and shared part of family and community life. It is only very recently, with the breakdown of community and the rise of complex and impersonal social institutions, that the duties of death have been delegated to professionals, to strangers.

Just 100 years ago, most people built their own houses, made their own clothes, and raised their own food. Little was delegated to others (except among the very wealthy, who had servants or slaves). But as our society entered the age of specialization, we stopped trusting ourselves to handle our own lives; we lost the ability to distinguish what is good to do for ourselves, and what we need others to help us do.

We became mobile, moving long distances from our family, often to crowded, urban housing. Home funerals and home burials grew more logistically difficult; we could no longer bury our relatives on our land. Slowly, death moved from our homes to hospitals and funeral parlors. Embalming was developed to preserve the body so that relatives living at long distances could travel to the funeral. The benefits of this approach came with a price: we became ignorant of the natural process of death.

Then, in 1963, Jessica Mitford wrote an exposé of the funeral business, *The American Way of Death*. Shortly afterward came Elisabeth Kubler-Ross's book *On Death and Dying*. Both books got us thinking and talking about death. In 1967, hospice, a movement to provide a supportive environment for the dying was founded in England by Cicely Saunders.

Still, death continues to be seen as an enemy in our culture. As Lewis Thomas wrote in *The Lives of a Cell*, "We will have to give up the notion that death is a catastrophe or detestable or avoidable or even strange. We will need to learn more about the cycling of life in the rest of the system and about our connection to the process. Everything that comes alive seems to be in trade for something that dies, cell for cell."

Not all cultures are like ours. To Buddhists, life is seen as preparation for the moment of death. Ram Dass, one of the most influential leaders of the consciousness movement, recalls someone saying to an Indian guru who was dying, "Don't go." The guru responded, "Where could I go?" If you are more than your physical body, death is just a transformational experience. You aren't going anywhere, you are simply parting company with your body.

Some cultures actually encourage preparation for death. In childhood, members of some Native American tribes learn how to perform a death chant, an instant centering technique to use whenever they are in a difficult situation: to help with the dangerous, the unknown; with death.

In Mexico on the Day of the Dead, people celebrate the nature of change by having picnics in nearby cemeteries. Children eat candy skulls and get paper skeletons which they blow apart with firecrackers. There are similar festivals in Hungary and Japan.

In Hasidic teaching, there is a tradition that helps people prepare for whatever might happen to them. As Stephen Levine explains, in *Who Dies*, "That kind of presence for our life is the perfect preparation for death. It means being open to whatever happens. Because if everything is okay except death, then eventually you notice that everything's okay but death and loss. And then everything's okay except death and loss and a bad pastrami sandwich. Then everything's okay but death, loss, a bad pastrami sandwich, and the plumber coming."

Back a generation or two in most families, decisions about death and dying were dictated largely by cultural and religious customs, not by personal choice. For many of us, this is still true. For others, the traditions have been obscured as our families have assimilated into secular society. For instance, a Jewish friend knew vaguely that after a death mourners are supposed to sit on stools and mirrors are covered—but she was not sure why.

Our families are also becoming more and more religiously complex. Take my family. My grandparents were practicing Orthodox Jews. My parents were Jewish but not religious. My husband was raised a Catholic. His parents are practicing Catholics. Our children attend a Jewish temple and a Catholic church.

What death customs will prevail? Should we follow cultural traditions, our own values and spiritual beliefs, or our parents' wishes? It would be equally appropriate for my family to sit *shiva*—or have a wake—depending on which side we wanted to please.

Since most of us in American society have been, to one degree or another, sheltered from death, the prospect of dealing with a parent's death can seem overwhelming. It certainly felt that way to me. With other difficult tasks in life, if what you are planning seems too hard, you can simply change your mind—decide not to build your house yourself or learn to run 10 miles a day. But your parent's death is not something you can simply choose to avoid or postpone.

Necessary Choices

Over time I came to see that my father's dying presented our family, and me personally, with a series of choices:

- What kind of medical treatment would he seek?

- How would we relate to his doctors and other care-givers?

- How often, and for how long, would I visit him?

- How much care would my mother and I be able to offer my father?

- How much emotional support?

- How would we take care of each other?

- What kind of funeral would be appropriate?

There were many, many other choices, many of them painful. As I became more familiar with the options that were available, I was better able to think intelligently about them, and to balance my father's needs against my own and those of my husband and children.

Each person faces a different set of choices in dealing with a parent's illness and death. These choices will be affected by your economic situation, your commitments to work and children, your geographical distance from your parent, your relationships with your siblings, and your own and your family's cultural traditions and personal values.

Most significantly, your choices will be shaped by your emotional history and relationship with your parents. Many people don't have the kind of relationships they would like to have with their parents; this book is not just for those who have good relationships. Whether your relationship has been wonderful or miserable or somewhere in between, once your parent becomes terminally ill, there are better and worse ways to relate. There are things to know that will make you more helpful, choices to be made, options to be explored.

You and your parent may enter this stage with complicated histories, past resentments, and contradictory feelings. But these do not have to get in the way of helping your parent if you are clear about what you can and want to do.

The loss of your parent will be hard on you, whether you have a good relationship or a difficult one; and if you are not prepared for your parent's death, it will be even harder. So this is a different sort of self-help book: it does not promise an easy path.

To be there for your parent, to get ready, you must do more than just collect information. You need to connect with others, and to get some sense of the different kinds of experiences that may await you. You need an armful of death and dying stories. This book is filled with such stories.

These are the stories of ordinary people, not saints or angels. They will give you some realistic images of what occurs between real parents and their adult children. Even so, I don't think that the stories will depress you; indeed, some may even make you laugh. They show that not only can you prepare for your parent's death, but you can be strengthened by your involvement in it.

Of course we don't want our parents to die. We don't want anyone to die, including ourselves. But a parent's death is a powerful, significant, and universal experience. Sometimes it's a last chance at a relationship. How you experience those few hours, weeks, or months can affect the rest of your life.

References

Kubler-Ross, E. (1969) *On Death and Dying*. New York: Macmillan.

Levine, S. (1982) *Who Dies*. New York: Anchor Books.

Ram Dass (1986) "Perspectives on Death: Address to the Staff at Bassett Hospital, Cooperstown, New York." Available from Hanuman Foundation Tape Library, 524 Anselmo Ave., #203, San Anselmo, CA 94960.

Catherine's Story of Her Mother's Death

Catherine is a real estate agent who lives on Shelter Island in New York. She grew up in Portland, Maine, where her father owned a furniture store. He drank heavily. Her mother, Betty, was a homemaker. She was chronically unhappy, and was both critical and demanding toward Catherine.

When Betty was 69, Catherine got a call from her father in Florida, where both parents had retired. Betty was in the hospital with pneumonia, "but they were starting to suspect she had something more serious," said Catherine. "I decided to go right down." Two days later, evidence was found of both lung cancer and bone cancer. Betty died, at home, 11 days after going into the hospital. Catherine was 45 at the time.

"My mother was such a guarded person, but our relationship kind of blossomed while she was in the hopitial. We became very close. She would talk to me a lot. And she was still able to joke. 'You know, I'm really doing very well—aren't you surprised?' She had been crazy her whole life and now, at a time when she really had a right to be nuts, she wasn't. We even talked at that level. I told her, 'You really pulled it together.'

"She had always been a hypochondriac. So there was some confirmation for her in this illness. She was finally really sick and getting all the attention she had looked for.

"My father was totally unable to deal with the seriousness of her illness. He was just running around frantically, doing nothing. So everything that my mohter would do was for me. She wanted my approval. She'd say to the nurse, 'I've promised Cathy I'd eat.'

"There were some very special moments. One day in the hospital, when I was feeling really exhausted, I climbed into bed with her. We were just lying there together. She was still lucid and we were talking. She loved me being there. At least I was able to feel I had been the best daughter while my mother was dying, even if I hadn't been the best daughter before that.

"Then we took her home to my parents' apartment. It was exhausting just getting her in the ambulance, on stretchers, into a wheelchair. It was an ordeal. Finally, we got her into bed. I had this little package of mints that she became attached to because they were mine. She had them and the only thing she really said after she got home was, 'I've still got my Tic Tacs' and she patted her pocket. She was never lucid after that. I had given her the mints and she just wouldn't be separated from them. I had them cremated with her—I did. I sent them with her. They had become her security.

"The family doctor prepared us very carefully for what was going to happen. He told us there would probably be a moment of utter panic, shortly before she died, when she would be begging us to keep her alive. And it happened.

"We were trying to give her opium with an eyedropper under her tongue, and she thought we were trying to kill her with it. She's screaming 'no!' and 'help me!', trying to push me away and get out of the bed. So we're trying to calm her when my father walks into the room, oblivious to her present state, and says, as if we were sitting on the porch drinking iced tea, 'Hi, Betty. How are you feeling, hon?' with a big smile on his face. She just turned to him and said, 'Who are you laughing at?' She had been totally incoherent up until this point. Clear as a bell, she says, 'Just get out of here.'

"A few minutes later I talked to him about what had happened. I asked him to consider how he would feel if he was in a panic, and someone walked into the room smiling at him. He said he didn't want her to see how upset he was. He had watched me. I would be crying outside the room, but when I came in to care for her, I would act very calm. He was just trying to do the same thing. I tried to point out that I wasn't smiling. It wasn't a smiling situation. But he was really too upset to understand.

"I didn't think she was going to be alive very much longer, and told him I thought he would feel terrible if he didn't go in and try to make some kind of peace with her—tell her that he loved her and say good-bye. My father did that and cried.

"That night, several hours later, while I was talking on the phone, my father called out, 'Cathy, I think she's dead.' I hung up and rushed into the bedroom. It was weird. I was very numb, but it wasn't as horrible as I thought it would be. She was lying there looking like she was resting.

"When the doctor came he was sweet. He hugged me. He was good with my father, too. Then the people came from hospice and took over. They threw away all my mother's medications. Then they asked us if we wanted to say good-bye.

"We each went into the bedroom and looked at her. The woman from hospice was with us. And she and I started talking. When I discovered she was planning to move up to New York City, I gave her my business card. And the guys from the funeral home are there—I mean, all of it's funny to them by now. They've done this a million times. And I thought, oh my god, I can't believe it. My mother's lying there dead, and I'm giving out my business cards. My grief was extremely controlled. I cried, but I also was functioning. I ws relieved when my mother died. I couldn't stand to see her breathing like she was. It was awful to watch. My chest hurt for two weeks after that.

"Meanwhile, my father's on the phone calling the funeral director in Maine, and we're all waiting for him because we don't think they should take the body out until he's seen her for the last time. And we hear my father giving the funeral director information for the obituary. 'There's my son, Carl, and his wife and children, and my daughter Catherine—she never got married.' I turn to the funeral guys and say, 'No one would have her' and we're all laughing. So there was all this mixture of laughing and crying."

2

The Fatal Diagnosis

Seven Guidelines To Help You Cope

Often you find out in a phone call. You hang up, but the words are still echoing in your head. They won't go away. "Your father is very ill."

"Your mother is in the hospital. It's serious. Come home right away."

When you learn that your parent is terminally ill, the ground shifts and you try to find your balance. You need to come to grips emotionally with what the news means to you, as well as make those difficult decisions about how best to help your parent and participate in his or her care.

In this chapter, I divide the process of adjustment and decision-making into seven guidelines:

- Take care of yourself: explore your feelings, protect your health, talk to friends

- Notice and acknowledge your fears, but hang in there

- As soon as possible, get together with your parent and the other members of your family

- Talk about death as openly as your parent's feelings will allow

- Make a family plan for dealing with the illness and death

- In dealing with treatment and care options, make your ideas known, but respect your parent's choices

- Be assertive with doctors, but don't alienate them

These guidelines are intended not as rules to be rigidly followed, but as a starting point to help put you on more solid ground.

Each guideline is followed by personal stories that will give you a glimpse of the variety of responses and approaches that are possible. There are also suggestions and exercises to help you cope with the extra physical, emotional, and mental stress of facing the loss of your parent.

Take Care of Yourself: Explore Your Feelings, Protect Your Health, Talk to Friends

Absorbing the news of a fatal diagnosis is never easy. But how you deal with it will set the tone for the remainder of your parent's life.

Begin by taking care of yourself. Talk to someone close to you about what's going on. Allow yourself to spend at least a few moments each day thinking about what is happening and how you're feeling. (Even if you don't plan it, this usually occurs anyway.)

A client told me, "I'm so preoccupied. I think about it all day at work. I can't stop myself. I'm starting to picture myself at the funeral. I can't seem to concentrate on my job or anything else."

You may find that you're berating yourself for having disregarded signs that your parent wasn't well. A friend of mine felt guilty because, a month before, she had gotten furious at her father. He had been helping her move to a new house and had dropped a lot of the boxes he was carrying. She had thought he was being careless. Now she realized that he had grown clumsy and uncoordinated because of his illness. Her father had always been strong and competent, someone she could rely on. She had avoided recognizing that he was becoming frail and ill.

Another friend thought about all the times he had noticed his father's hands shaking, and had said nothing. Maybe if his father had gotten to a doctor sooner....

A social worker I know had just returned from vacation when her father called from the hospital. She remembers feeling grateful to have had such a nice holiday, because she knew that it would be a long time before she would enjoy another one.

Don't try to act as if nothing has happened. You are starting to experience the emotional impact of losing your parent; this is your time to prepare for the actual death. Each time you wrestle in your mind with the diagnosis, each time you visit, you become more accustomed to the idea that your parent is going to die. It's like easing yourself slowly into an icy ocean. Little by little, your body adjusts to the cold, so that when you are finally submerged, you've adjusted. The shock and the danger aren't as great as they would have been if you'd simply been tossed overboard.

Remember, there is no "correct" reaction to the news of a parent's illness. Reactions are as varied as individual relationships. If your mother or father has been a burden, there can actually be a sense of relief—an end in sight. The owner of a cheese-and-wine store in Boston told me about his father, a once-famous sportswriter who had become an alcoholic. His behavior was a source of public humiliation to his family. "I remember feeling a tremendous relief when I got the call that he was ill and wasn't expected to live. It had been a nightmare for all of us. I worried about myself for a while. Why didn't I feel worse? How can you feel glad your father's dying?"

Try not to censor or judge your feelings. For now it's simply important to feel and accept your emotions, whatever they are.

Since most people will be in very unfamiliar territory during this time, they'll need help—someone who's been there before. One woman told me, "I was operating in an area that was a total mystery to me. It was my friend Jane, whose father had died of cancer the year before, who helped me the most. She took me step by step so I would know what to expect, what I ought to be doing and looking out for."

Tips for Staying Healthy in Times of Crisis

Be as conscientious as you can about eating. Have regular mealtimes. Eat easy-to-digest, nourishing food. If you have less time to cook than usual, make sure that you aren't existing on junk food.

Some easy-to-eat, easy-to-prepare meals:

- Baked potato with grated cheese
- Vegetable cut-ups and cheese
- Peanut butter and jelly sandwich on whole wheat bread
- Sliced apples and cheese
- Bagel and cream cheese
- Yogurt and fruit
- Cereal, milk, and fruit

Avoid added sugar, artificial colorings, and preservatives, if you can. Tell friends that this is a good time to invite you over for meals (if you feel up to it, and a bit of normal socializing will probably be good for you). If fast food is your only option, avoid anything fried, and take advantage of the salad bars that most fast-food places now offer.

Avoid:

- Drinking more than two cups of caffeinated coffee a day

- All foods and drinks that are high in sugar and caffeine (12 ounces of Pepsi contains 10 teaspoons of sugar)

- Eating while driving or on the run

- Cigarettes, drugs, and alcohol

This is a time when you need to be operating at 100 percent. Drink lots of water; eat lots of fresh fruits, vegetables, and whole grains. Don't skimp on sleep—you'll probably need at least eight hours a day.

Many people react to the illness and suffering of a loved one by running themselves ragged—perhaps in an attempt to prove to themselves and others the depth of their feeling. And yet making *yourself* sick will not do anything to help your parent; on the contrary, it will just make you less effective as a helper, and less available as a companion. The depth of your feelings will be best expressed directly in conversation with your parent and others.

Don't try to do too much. Always leave yourself extra time, at least 15 minutes, between appointments. This is time you may need to use to take a few deep breaths, eat a nutritious snack, or even catch 30 winks. Treat yourself like an athlete in training: after all, the situation is making extraordinary demands on your body, heart, and mind.

Notice and Acknowledge Your Fears, But Hang in There

For some people, getting involved in the process of a parent's death will seem easy and natural. For others, it may take an act of will to override your anxieties, or a great deal of support to get beyond the fear that you will prove inadequate in the situation.

If you feel overwhelmed by anxiety and a sense of being unprepared, you are not alone. One client of mine admitted that he was too frightened and sad to spend much time in the hospital room with his mother. He was someone who couldn't stand seeing anyone upset or suffering, and feared that he would break down and cause his mother even more pain.

Many people worry that their feelings are somehow wrong. Seeing a parent become frail and weak, or demanding and irrational, can elicit feelings of revulsion and anger. "It was horrible, at first" one man told me, "to see my father lying in bed, partially paralyzed from a stroke, drooling, needing help to perform even the simplest task. This was a man who at 80 had been able to cut down trees. It scared and disgusted me. I felt he was pathetic. I didn't know how to relate to him."

One of the most common fears is that, faced with the pain of the situation, you'll fall apart and make things even worse. You don't want to do anything wrong or make things more difficult for your parent—you reason that maybe it would be better just to wait outside until it's over. So you avoid the subject, avoid contact, deny the reality. But such a strategy rarely makes things any easier, either for you or your parent. One college friend, years after his mother's death, still couldn't talk about the subject. He had been too busy with his high-pressure government job—and too frightened—to make himself available when his mother was ill and dying. He hired care, but afterwards there was no one he could hire to assuage his feelings of guilt and remorse. He was stuck with these.

Another man I interviewed remembered thinking, "My sister can handle this better that I can." And he was right; she could. But she worked through her feelings of grief within a year, while he was still preoccupied and upset over his parent's death three years later. It's not a simple question of who is best able to cope with the immediate situation; what you do or don't do will dramatically affect how you feel for a long time after-wards.

When I first heard the news about my father, I remember feeling so overwhelmed that I couldn't think straight, and so depressed that I felt numb. But I moved on from that place, and so will you.

Becky Donovan got a telephone call one night telling her that her father was in a hospital in Florida, fatally ill.

> *I went right down there, and it was the first time in my whole life that my parents were not at the airport to meet me. I knew my life as a child, where they were taking care of me, was over; and I was afraid I wasn't going to be able to cope.*

Most people initially react with fear to the news of their parent's illness. One particularly hearty woman told me, "I never really put aside my fears; I just started doing things for my mother. I just did what had to be done. And there was some-thing enriching about the experience, about encountering dif-ficult and hard feelings and still taking care of business."

People find all sorts of ways to cope. Another friend told me, "It was interesting how easy and comfortable I began to feel taking care of my father. His body was a mess. But if it doesn't feel like the body is all there is, then seeing it decay isn't so horrible."

One man I spoke to felt very anxious and uncomfortable when his father could no longer talk clearly. So when he went to visit, he would avoid making conversation, and instead focused on doing things for his dad. He would hold his father's hand, mop his forehead, cut his toenails, and, if his father seemed up to it, he would read to him from the newspaper.

Your parent's attitude will affect how easy or hard a time you have. When my 76-year-old uncle had a malignant growth removed from his cheek, he went around telling everyone that he'd had "Open Mouth Surgery," and returned to work as soon as he was able. He wasn't about to obsess that his illness might be terminal. My friend's mother, on the other hand, called her long distance twice a day for months after she became ill, unable to allow herself—or her daughter—to focus on anything else.

The most difficult part of this challenge is to accept your own feelings and attitudes as well as those of your parent. All of these just are what they are: don't waste precious time at the end trying to manipulate them into some preconceived idea of what they *should* be. Notice, accept, and then work with what you have.

During the final six months of my father's illness, I had butterflies in my stomach. From out of nowhere, in they would fly. It was as if there were some underground reservoir of fear that would suddenly overflow from whatever solid container it was held in, and I would feel afraid.

What I found most helpful was to try to translate anxiety into energy. Exercise. Write it into your weekly schedule in ink, not pencil, so it is a nonerasable activity: three times a week, minimum. Walk 45 minutes to an hour. Run. Go to the gym. Take a yoga class.

Try using routine activities, like washing your car or vacuuming, to work away anxious feelings.

Relax. You're repressing a lot of anguish, trying to act okay in front of your parent. You also need time away with other people who are healthy and vital.

Rosa stayed close by in Florida while her father was dying, far away from her friends and support system. She found that it helped her to go shopping. Hunting for bargains proved to be a good way for Rosa to relax and get away.

Whatever the activity—shopping, going out for dinner, playing tennis, exercising, making love—everyone seems to have moments when the contradiction between what they are doing and what's happening to their parent feels overwhelming.

One woman recalls sitting in a beautiful restaurant, laughing, relaxed, having a delicious meal with her uncle. She actually succeeded in forgetting her sadness for the moment. When the sadness returned, though, she confused it with guilt. Would her father be more likely to live if she stayed with him constantly? Would she be more able to nurture him if she stopped nurturing herself?

Even though it may seem counterintuitive, the answer to both questions is no. Don't confuse compassion with martyrdom. Your life, and its continuance, deserve as much care and respect as the fact that your parent is dying. Part of your responsibility to your parent is to continue living, and to live as well and richly as you possibly can.

As Soon as Possible, Get Together with Your Parent and the Other Members of Your Family

The sooner you can make a connection with your parent, the easier this time will be for both of you. If at all possible, this should be done in person; but a phone call is better than nothing.

Tell your parents or parent whatever you can about how you're feeling, and explore their feelings, too. Are they ready to talk about death? Find out how much trust they're putting in doctors. Find out how accepting they are of the diagnosis. Assess what you think their approach to care options will be.

When a neighbor of mine learned that his father had liver cancer, he arranged a big family dinner. Afterwards they all went to see a play. Although everyone involved heard the news, it was still a very cheerful evening. They shared a good time. "I felt it was important to pull our family together. My father had come close to dying about eight times. And I had been very involved on all of those occasions. I had a sense that he was almost invincible, so part of me denied that he would actually die. At the same time, he did seem really vulnerable now."

When another uncle was diagnosed with terminal cancer, my cousins flew to Florida within a week to visit him. One cousin lived in New Jersey, the other in Colombia, South America. Although it might have been months, or years, before he died, coming together right away gave them time together with my uncle while he was still feeling well enough to enjoy their company. On this first visit, they did not bring their young children. This way my cousins would have no extra demands made on their time. The next visit, a month away, was planned to include the grandchildren.

Just because your parent is close to death doesn't mean that all your disagreements will magically disappear or that your personalities will dramatically change; but it helps if you can work on your relationship, trying as hard as you can to take care of any unfinished business. Unfinished business can add to the pain later on. Several people I interviewed felt that their parent's death was easier for them to accept simply because they had been able to express their feelings of love.

Even if you and your parent have had a poor relationship all along, the last scene can change the whole story. Not everyone I interviewed had a close, easy, relationship with their parent. But many found that when they infused the last stage with love and caring, these positive feelings also seemed to affect the past. One woman told me that the loving relationship that developed when her father became terminally ill did much to heal the wounds from the past. "Finally all our past history, all the hurt and anger, just melted away."

Many people live long distances from their families. This can raise questions that create turmoil and have no easy answer.

- How often should you visit?

- How can you best be involved?

- Where can you find help you can trust?

- Should you take a leave of absence from your job?

- How do you decide what you need to handle in person, and what you can take care of by telephone?

The answers to these questions must be drawn from your own individual situation: financial constraints, your health, family commitments, and the demands of your profession will all play a role. Try to make room in your life for this unwanted and unexpected event. But recognize that timing and outside commitments will affect your ability to help. If you are nursing a baby, dirt poor, about to have bypass surgery, or just starting a new job with deadlines and responsibilities that cannot be changed, you may find the long distances between you and your parent to be practically insurmountable.

One friend of mine was nine months pregnant with her third child when her mother, who lived an eight-hour drive away, had a heart attack. She could not rush to her side and stay with her. She couldn't even visit. But she used the telephone to stay in touch daily with her siblings, the hospital staff, and her mom.

If you can, visit as soon as possible. Plan ahead of time what you want to accomplish. You may want to use the telephone to arrange an appointment with your parent's doctor before the visit. Make a list of all the support systems you'll need to connect with while you are in your parent's area:

- What kind of shopping and housekeeping help is available?

- What taxi services are available, and what are their rates?

- What's considered to be the best local medical facility? Do they have a palliative care unit?

- Is there a local Emergency Response System (ERS)? This will be particularly crucial if your parent lives alone. An ERS—usually a private agency—can be accessed by people who need it by pulling a cord attached to the wall or pushing a signaling device worn around the neck. These will cause an alarm to go off at a control center, where staff will either alert the manager of your parent's building or dispatch an ambulance.

- Is there a geriatric case manager in the area? These are trained psychotherapists or social workers who make home visits. They can help with a lot of the problems that you won't be able to resolve by yourself over the telephone.

If you can't visit, for whatever reason, stay in touch. Telephone often. Find ways to make your parent feel loved and well cared for, even from afar.

One woman sent her father a card every day. A frugal man, he told her not to buy cards and waste money. So every day, she sat down and made him a card, taping a quarter inside of it. She did that for a year, until he died. He saved every card she sent.

You may also want to discuss with your parent the option of moving closer to where you live. Again, this will depend on your parent's individual situation, including the location of other family members involved, and his or her entrenchment in the community. Don't rip your parent away from a tight network of supportive friends unless you know that you have the time and energy to provide that support yourself. Be realistic about what your parent needs, as well as about what you're able to give. This is a big decision—seek the advice of others if you feel unsure about what to offer. The final decision about whether or not to move—if *you're* willing—will rest with your parent.

Talk About Death as Directly as Your Parent's Feelings Will Allow

The fatal diagnosis can be the moment when it becomes painfully clear how unprepared you are to deal with death. Death may not be a subject you have ever talked openly about in your family. You may not even use the word ("So and so *passed away.*" "I am so sorry she's *gone.*"). A friend of mine, whose mother had just died, felt very annoyed by a neighbor's comment, "I heard you lost your mother." She responded with a sarcasm that pained her later on, "Yes, we were at the vegetable stand in the grocery store, and I turned around and she was gone!"

I'm an advocate of talking openly about everything, including death. A subject that's whispered about, or kept secret, becomes more awful. Nonetheless, this is the time to be acutely sensitive to our parent's needs and the ways in which he or she will feel most comfortable talking about illness and death.

My father was unwilling to talk openly about death until the very final stage of his illness. I think he wanted to remain hopeful and believe that he wasn't really going to die. He knew that he had brain cancer, but denying that it was fatal helped him enjoy the time he had left.

How I dealt with the knowledge of his illness by myself and among my friends was different from how I broached the subject with him. For myself, I was open about what was going on, and kept reading books about death and dying as a way to prepare. But outside of sharing some Stephen Levine stories with my father about the possibilities of life after death, and trying to help him feel less afraid, I followed his lead and did not discuss the subject with him openly.

Susan's father never talked about his death either—not to anybody. She remembers him saying just a few days before he died, "I'm going to quit smoking, because I want to live as long as I can." He never accepted that he was dying, and Susan and her mother and brothers respected that. But they at least tried to be honest with one another about what was happening.

On a home visit to a man with only a few days left to live, a grief counselor tried to help him talk with his wife about his funeral arrangements and will. The dying man's response was, "Excuse me, Miss—I don't want to hurt your feelings, but you're scaring me."

Sometimes it's only possible to acknowledge death in-
directly. A friend's mother in her final days focused on what
would become of her property and possessions. For years afterwards, my friend was furious about this. Why had her mother
devoted their last moments together to obsessing about material
things? For many people, discussing the fate of possessions is
an indirect way of acknowledging death. "What will you do
with these expensive cups and saucers?" can be translated as,
"Take care of yourself, take care of my things. I want you to
have and enjoy my possessions. I want to help you be all right
without me." If your family has difficulty talking about death,
you may find this ritual of discussing possessions to be a useful
starting point.

On the other hand, talking about money, possessions, and
wills in some families is completely taboo. You have to be the
judge of what will fly and what won't with your parents. Every
family is different.

Many people I interviewed found tremendous relief in being able to talk openly with their parents. But all of them who
did so had parents who seemed able to face and accept death.
Their parents set the tone.

One woman's mother wrote her daughter a note when she
was on a respirator, saying "I want to die." Her father wanted
to hide the note, afraid of the doctors seeing it. But the note
itself—her mother's clear wishes—made it much easier to go to
the doctors and give them instructions about no "heroic efforts."
This was a case in which one parent's wishes had to be balanced
against the other's. "Without that note," said the daughter, "I
would have felt guilty."

I heard of another situation in which both parents were
having serious health problems. They sent a memo in legal language to each of their six children. The memo went over their
wishes, and asked for general feedback as well as a list of the
particular possessions each child wanted. The friend who told
me this story was pleased that her parents were so considerate,
but a little stunned by the method they had chosen. And yet

the memo opened up the subject of the parents' death for the entire family, allowing them to consider it in practical terms for the first time.

You may be one of the lucky ones with a straightforward and communicative parent. After Carol received news of the seriousness of her father's illness, he said to her openly, "I'm not afraid to die." Carol recalls:

> *Because there was no need to try to hide anything of his condition from him, it was easy to talk to the doctors. I had the feeling that the doctors and nurses appreciated being able to be so straightforward with everybody involved. They told us we asked the same questions a lot of families and patients ask, but it was easier to talk to us about what was actually physically happening, because there didn't seem to be any fear.*

Openness about the gravity of your parent's illness is generally the best policy. It is helpful for people to have time, when possible, to talk with their families, resolve difficulties, express love, and deal with financial details. However, even denial and repression can sometimes enhance your parent's last days (as was the case with my father); hope has proven to be an aid in the recovery of countless individuals. Each situation is different, and calls for an individual response. Unfortunately, there is no magic formula.

How your parent finds out is very important. There is a very fine line between respectful honesty and devastating bluntness. One woman was at the doctor's office with her father when he asked what would happen if they couldn't take the tumor out of his throat. The doctor replied that he would probably live about six months. It had not occurred to either father or daughter before that the surgery might not work. Both of them just sat there unable to speak. When they left, her father asked if she had heard what the doctor said. When she acknowledged that she had, they went to one of their favorite bars, had a drink, and talked. Her mother later said that if the daughter hadn't been along on this particular trip to the doctor, the father probably would have gone out and killed himself.

If it seems like the right approach for your parent, you might try saying something like this: "You have an illness that's generally considered to be fatal. I want you to know, so you don't postpone what you would like to have happen while you're alive. It's not at all certain you *will* die from this illness, or when you'll die. People have miraculous, unexplainable re-coveries. New treatments are being discovered every day, and there's even the possibility of a cure being found. But it only seems fair for you to know all the possibilities, so that you can get done what you need to get done. I'll be here to help you in any way I can."

At all costs, you should avoid apologies and long discussions when your parent is feeling badly. Avoid manipulative comments like, "I want you to have that surgery," or "Please—do it for me," or "Don't talk like that!" Try to remember that your parent's feelings deserve to be honored, no matter how "wrong" they may seem to you or anyone else.

There are several issues that it would be useful to discuss with your parent if he or she is willing to talk openly.

- Given a choice, where would he prefer to die? At home, in a hospital, or in a nursing home?

- Does she want a funeral or memorial service? If so, what sort of service would most please her? Is there a particular person she'd like to have officiate? Is there particular music she'd like to have played or sung?

- Does he want to be buried or cremated? If he wants to be cremated, where would he like the ashes to be stored or scattered?

- Does she want to give away any of her healthy organs? (If so, particular paperwork must be filled out. You can get more information from your parent's doctor.)

Obviously, such questions must be asked with sensitivity and tact. You may not want to ask them all at once. Again, try to stay attuned to your parent's desire and capacity to talk at a given time.

Make a Family Plan for Dealing with the Illness and Death

Making a family plan is one of the most important things you can do—and one of the most difficult.

This is a time when you can't or shouldn't have to function as an isolated person. If you have siblings, divide up the work. "It's fair to share" should be an overriding principle. One person may be able to handle buying groceries or fixing meals; another could oversee the medical care and deal with legal and financial problems. Who is good at what? Who is available? If you are an only child, then friends and neighbors, as well as social service agencies, can be called on to help.

If your family can't settle its differences (or at least get them out of the way for a while), enlist the help of a social worker. Hospice programs, and hospitals and nursing homes often have trained professionals on staff who know how to facilitate communication and cooperation within families. If not, they can give you referrals to other professionals who can help.

Several people I interviewed held family meetings, sometimes with their parents, sometimes without them. At these meetings, they would make schedules, divide up the work, discuss problems, and share feelings. This prevented hidden resentments from festering. Interestingly, when you talk about negative feelings, some of their intensity is diminished. If you're the *only* family member, find a network of friends to help you. Writing about your feelings can help put them in perspective and make them less overwhelming.

This is a time made easier or harder by the way in which your family deals with the responsibilities that emerge. Sometimes family dynamics can create difficulties; at other times they can add strength.

It's easy to become resentful if you feel that you're getting stuck with all the difficult tasks. Kathryn, at first, remembers complaining to herself that she had to do everything.

> *Then I realized everyone can't play the same role. I was single and could deal with the responsibility. Once I stopped expecting my brother to be any different we got very close. We even cried together.*

Another friend had always found it easy to tolerate her brother's lackadaisical approach to life. But now, with a seriously ill parent, she recognized that it would be harder to be understanding. "Was my brother going to be a help, someone I'd have to take care of, or someone I'd have to get rid of?"

Don't be surprised when family conflicts arise. A client of mine clashed with her mother over how to care for her father. "She would allow my dad to lie in bed all day—fed him breakfast in his room. I thought she should motivate him, but instead she babied him. We ended up having muffled arguments outside my father's bedroom."

Someone else found herself in competition with her mother. She would often stay at the hospital overnight, sitting next to her father's bed. "My mother was really angry about that. She didn't understand. She wanted me to go home with her. She couldn't stay up with him, so she felt guilty. She'd say, 'He doesn't know you're there. Why are you staying?' It made everything harder and added to the stress."

Several other people I talked to described feelings of competition, often with brothers and sisters. One woman told me, "I wanted to feel like I was being the best possible child. I remember worrying, 'Am I doing enough, am I there enough, am I coping as well as my brothers?' I had this fear that I wasn't going to compare well with them."

Sometimes conflicts arise within families over medical strategies. One client I worked with felt enormous anger toward her mother for rigidly following the doctor's directions, keeping her father on a cancer diet long after it was clear that he would not recover. "I told her to let him have what he wants. She made me sick, stuck on her cancer cookbook. She also pushed him to take chemotherapy when I thought he should be left alone. But I kept quiet. She lived with 'it' and him all the time. I didn't."

Whether you're on your own, or working in conjunction with your family, there are important legal and financial concerns that need to be dealt with.

- Make sure that your parent has a will. Most people can write one themselves, without the assistance of lawyers. There are self-help books, like Denis Clifford's, *Simple Will Book: How to Prepare a Legally Valid Will* (Rev. ed. Berkeley, CA: Nolo Press, 1990), that contain sample wills. There are also computer software programs you can purchase for writing a will. Last will and testament forms are available in some states, at office supply and stationery stores.

  However, if there are complicating factors regarding property and money, or if family members don't get along, it would be best to consult with a lawyer who is skilled in estate planning.

- Make sure that you know where the will is being kept. Many people keep their will in a safe deposit box, even though this is not the best place. In some states, safe deposit boxes are sealed immediately upon death. A secure place in the home, such as a fireproof metal box, would be better. If your parent has a trusted lawyer, the will can be left on file at his or her office. If you need a lawyer, and can't get a personal recommendation, call your local bar association. Mention specific concerns. One person I interviewed found a lawyer who made home visits (her mother lived far away and was housebound).

- Ask your parent if he or she wants a *living will*. This is a directive to doctors describing what medical treatments would be acceptable. Your parent can be very specific (for instance, no cardiac resuscitation, no life support systems when death is imminent, and so on).

    Living will forms can be obtained from the Society for the Right To Die, 250 West 57th St., New York, NY 10107.

    A *durable power of attorney for health care* (DPA), also called *medical power of attorney* or "medical proxy," is also important. Your parent can authorize you, or someone else, to make medical decisions on his or her behalf, if your parent becomes incapacitated. It is best to consult with an attorney in order to arrange a DPA.

- Ask your parent for another form of durable power of attorney in the form of written authorization allowing you to pay bills and manage your parent's property if your parent is unable to fill this role. It is best to consult with an attorney for this DPA as well.

- Make a list of key documents—insurance policies, property titles, passbooks for bank accounts, past tax records, deeds to cemetery plots—and find out where they are kept. Of course, you needn't bother your parent with these details unless he or she is unmarried or lives alone.

Use discretion in obtaining this information, and be sensitive to the feelings of your siblings and others who may be involved. Emotions run high on these occasions, and many a family has experienced terrible rifts concerning a dying parent's last wishes, or the disposition of his or her will. Part of your family meeting should entail reaching an agreement about who asks what questions. If you're the designated one, here are some approaches you might tailor to your parent's individual situation.

- I'd like to help you take care of these legal matters, so that everything gets done the way you'd like it to be.

- Let's take care of this now, if you feel up to it. I'd like to be able to get as much settled as possible while you can still make your wishes known.

- It's important for me to know the location of all your key documents, so nothing gets forgotten. I have a list here that we can fill in together.

In Dealing with Treatment and Care Options, Make Your Ideas Known, But Respect Your Parent's Choices

A number of people I interviewed said that their parents wanted to be taken care of by doctors, and only felt comfortable following the directions of their doctor. Other parents participated actively in their own care, asking questions and learning the details of what was going on. By assessing how your parent wants to handle the illness, you can help in the way he or she most wants to be helped. This doesn't mean that you can't suggest alternatives, ask your parents to consider different approaches, or raise questions for them to think about. But do it as a kind and gentle assistant rather than as a boss or stage manager.

When Shea came back from visiting her father in the hospital and told her friends about his illness, she got lots of advice about what to do.

The first suggestion I got was to have my father go to a special clinic where he'd get the best of care. So I went back home with that advice and found out early that was the wrong thing to do. I was 37 then, I was grown up. But to doubt the doctors that my parents had chosen was to doubt them and their judgment at a time when they already felt powerless. They needed to know they were in charge of some things.

I mean, I had all these ideas about different diets, all these alternatives and visualization techniques...and it just didn't fit with who they were. I would have liked my father's death to be a "Stephen Levine" death, but that comes from my life, not my parents' life. And so I learned fast to back off. At other stages of our relationship, if I had any idea in opposition to my parents, I never backed off. That was the fun part. But I could see that to push my ideas over theirs—this was not the time. So I took the role of simply going with my father when he had to visit the doctor.

Becky knew that her mother, who had been a nurse all her adult life, wanted to be the one to make all the decisions. So Becky was careful:

I didn't want to zoom in, like I'd heard from a lot of people they had done—and it hadn't worked out too well, and caused a lot of family conflict. My father had several different specialists, and each doctor would come in, say something, then leave. Nobody ever explained to us exactly what was going on. On looking back, maybe it would have been better if I could have been more assertive— asked more questions, demanded other answers.

Gretchen's father, a vigorous man, became sick and needed to go to the hospital: he had serious heart problems. When the doctors wanted to do an angiogram, he refused, leaving the hospital. He was convinced, Gretchen remembers, that somehow they would take something from him. He joked, "If

I stay, I know I'll lose a leg." He told his family, "I don't want to be in that hospital anymore. I'll do everything I can as an outpatient, and if that doesn't work, well, good-bye." Gretchen's father clearly knew his feelings and what would be acceptable to him, and that made it easier for the rest of the family. They simply followed his lead.

Toby had a very good relationship with his mother. Her open and sometimes humorous approach to her illness made it easier for him to take a more assertive role. He knew that he couldn't push her to do something she didn't want to, but she did value his suggestions.

>We had seen what the traditional doctors had offered, and I was really hoping my mother would look at some alternatives. I suggested that we see another type of doctor to see what they would have to say. I pointed out, it was ultimately her decision what she was going to do. She agreed, even though she didn't believe an alternative was going to be much help.
>
>She ended up working with alternative doctors, who made use of a macrobiotic diet, and various other holistic approaches, along with antibiotics. We spent an unimaginable four hours at a stretch with these doctors. We had spent that much time with the surgeons—but most of it was in the waiting room. She followed the alternative program to the letter for almost a year. Although it never stopped the growth in her mouth, her blood pressure came down, she had energy and optimism, and much less pain at the very end than if she would have if she had followed the Western medicine path.

In my first phone call to my father's oncologist, I asked about the best and worst cases with my father's diagnosis the doctor had seen. He told me that one patient had died within a month; another was still alive a year and a half later. That gave me a realistic range, and helped me make decisions about when to plan visits with my father. But it was my father himself who opted for radiation and steroids instead of surgery. I kept quiet, even though I thought this was the wrong approach.

Choosing a Hospital

People typically give more consideration to their choice of a hotel than they give to choosing a hospital. Often they don't choose: they simply go where their doctor sends them (or to the facility where their doctor has hospital privileges).

Depending on your commitment to a particular doctor, and your geographic location, you may not *have* much choice. But, given some latitude, here are some factors that you and your parents might want to take into consideration.

- If possible, choose a hospital that trains interns and residents, and is affiliated with a medical school. The quality of care is bound to be more sophisticated at such a facility.

- It's preferable to choose a hospital that has a palliative care unit—a special section in the hospital for people who are dying. These units are less inclined than a general treatment facility to put your parent through unnecessary laboratory tests and treatment.

Susan remembers the night her father was transferred to palliative care.

> *The ward clerk called ahead to say we were coming. The nurses had made coffee and showed us around. It was something like a two-to-one patient-nurse ratio. They were just sitting there waiting to talk to my father and me. It was like going home, and the only good experience we had in the hospital.*

Remember—hospitalized patients have rights. They have the right to privacy, the right to refuse to be seen by those not directly involved in their care, the right to be informed, the right to refuse treatment. Your parent may be too ill to make use of this information, but you can be his or her advocate. Many hospitals now have a professional patient advocate on staff. This person can help advise you and your parents of your rights.

Be Assertive with Doctors, But Don't Alienate Them

Doctors' responses to fatal illness reflect the incredible contradictions inherent in their work. Oncologists especially have to deal constantly with enormous ambivalence. On the one hand, they want to be supportive and cheerful, knowing the importance of hope in helping people recover; yet many of their patients die. So the doctors come in to the hospital room and say things like, "Good, cough it up," or "Eat this food and in a few days you'll be feeling better." Often these bright and optimistic statements are at odds with what's really going on. False cheer can be depressing to patients, families, and physicians.

Then, when it's obvious that the chemotherapy or the surgery hasn't produced a remission, it's not uncommon for the doctor simply to stop coming around.

It's been observed that most Western doctors know how to fight for a patient's life, but don't know anything about allowing a patient to die. One doctor I spoke with pointed out that there were virtually no courses in his medical school on death and dying, nothing to help him understand loss and grief. "Not much death education goes on anywhere for health professionals. It's not surprising that most of us are eager to avoid the subject."

Many doctors are caring, considerate people who are overwhelmed by the task of caring for people who become very ill and die. It takes practice to learn how to communicate with doctors, to ask questions until the answers make sense. It helps to give them a clear sense of how much you want to know—and whether that's the same as what your parent wants to know.

I found that being very involved, and developing my own relationship with my father's doctor helped me a lot; it also helped me assist my father in making decisions. After getting my father's permission, I called his doctor with a list of questions I had written down beforehand. The doctor was respectful and made time for my phone calls. I would always call to make an appointment beforehand, speaking with his nurse, to explain what I wanted: to set up a time when the doctor would be available to speak to me at some length on the telephone.

One man I interviewed described how confusing and complicated the choices for his mother's care appeared to be. He did not agree with the doctors' approach to illness—burn it, cut it out, destroy it—and he admits that he would not have chosen these methods if the choice had been left up to him. And yet his mother lived for 12 years in relatively good health after choosing disfiguring surgery for her neck cancer and radiation and chemotherapy for subsequent cancers. The interventions ended up giving her many productive years.

Another person, a nurse, told me that when her father's bone cancer reached his brain, and he was unconscious after having been in severe pain, the first thing the surgeon suggested was an operation to remove the brain tumor. She wanted to know why—what purpose would it serve? He said that it would restore her father to consciousness. She remembers thinking how it was as if the doctor was going out of his way to restore her father's agony. And yet the surgeon was only doing what he'd been trained to do. Naturally, the family refused the operation.

What if a doctor is unwilling to say how sick your parent is, or what to expect? One woman told me, "When my father was in the hospital, the doctors never explained exactly what was going on. Nobody ever gave us any facts, or said how much time we were dealing with." In a similar situation, you could ask to speak with the head nurse; or seek out the hospital's patient advocate. In a doctor's office, you can request to see your parent's chart, provided that you have the appropriate permission. Your parent has the legal right to have access to all the information in his or her medical records. Assert this right if you need to.

During the last stage of my father's illness, he had a seizure and was hospitalized. During his stay in the hospital, the doctor came to know me, as well as my father. He could see that I understood that my father wasn't going to recover. So when my father was about to be discharged, I asked the doctor what I should do if there was another seizure. He answered honestly: I could bring my father back to the emergency room, in which case he would most likely die in the hospital. The alternative was to keep him at home and let him die there. The doctor would never have given this information to my father, who was still hoping to recover.

For John, it was only after his father's death that he felt educated enough to make good decisions.

> *If anyone else in my family ever develops cancer, we will certainly be very skeptical about treatment. If they had a cancer that was reasonably well confined, we would of course want to have treatment; but if it was generalized cancer, we would not. I learned that there are three different areas of cancer specialty—all have their own biases and distortions and are inclined to overtreat patients. In looking back, I'm struck by how the medical people could make decisions that were so poor in terms of my father's well-being—the oncologist who recommended the chemotherapy that made my father so ill; the primary care physician who was going to let him starve and not give him an I.V. It showed me how critically important it is that we do our own thinking.*

With all the decisions to make, it's easy to lose perspective on the larger issues. Susan remembers:

My family got overly involved in daily decisions. Should he have the operation? Yes, he should. Now he has to recover from the operation. By the time he does, another month's gone by and you move to another crisis. And you have to make another decision. Should he or shouldn't he have the chemotherapy? You forget day to day that the person is dying. You forget about resolving issues with your family members, because you have these immediate crises. Maybe that's a blessing—immediate kinds of problems to solve instead of sitting around and thinking, Oh my god, my father's dying. What am I going to do?

There is no shortage of disturbing stories about doctors' attitudes. One woman noticed that her father's doctor usually addressed his comments only to her brother, who came to the hospital from work wearing a suit and tie. She and another brother, dressed more casually, were ignored.

Another woman went so far as to wear seductive outfits to the hospital. She remembers thinking, "If the doctor is attracted to me, maybe his interest will translate into good care for my father."

Rosa's experiences with doctors were horrible. "You feel like, when they talk to you, they're condescending to give you their time. They're always impatient. I felt helpless with them. But I loved being in the waiting room with other people. We could commiserate together."

A sense of humor can sometimes help break through a doctor's arrogance. One woman was greeted by her father's doctor, "Hello, Margot, nice to meet you, I'm Dr. Rogers." She exclaimed in a loud and surprised manner, "I've never met someone whose parents named them Doctor. I've heard of Major Major but never Doctor Doctor." She wanted to give him a message: Don't talk down to me. Don't call me by my first name and expect me to refer to you by your title. (Of course, if you can think of a more diplomatic way to get this message across, you should. You can ask directly if he or she would feel comfortable being on a first-name basis; or you could say that you'd be more comfortable if the doctor addressed you as Ms. Smith or Mr. Jones.)

The medical profession is beginning to respond to the public's messages. Birth centers have been created in hospitals to provide a more humane and healthy approach to labor and delivery; soon we may also see dying centers. A new model of health care is emerging. Mel Moore, an oncologist and director of hospice in Atlanta, told me:

> *I try to be careful about being judgmental. Recently, I pressured a friend to keep her father at home when she didn't want to. I imposed on her my vision of what should happen. I did it as a friend, not a doctor. But that doesn't make it any better.*
>
> *My job is to give my patients a vision, not to tell them what to do. Options, not solutions. I encourage the families I work with to get as much information as they can before making decisions about treatment and care. Everyone has the right to expect emotional as well as technical competence.*

The physician treating Catherine's mother showed just that kind of competence. When his patient asked him how long he thought she would live, he answered honestly: she might have three weeks. He told her that she could fight what was going to happen, but it would be horrible. She was going to die. The disease was so advanced that there was no way to fight it off. And if she got into fighting, she would be miserable. He suggested that she accept it, and try to enjoy herself and her family as much as possible. Although Catherine's mother never really had time to make those choices—she drifted into a coma shortly afterwards—Catherine felt that the whole family had been helped by the doctor's open and clear approach. Instead of spending time trying to deny what was happening, they could all concentrate on making her mother feel as well loved and comfortable as possible.

When my father was in the hospital, the resident, who knew that my father had been a pharmacist, asked him, "What would you like me to prescribe for your constipation?" That doctor understood how helpful it would be to my father, now weak and frail, to feel that he was being given some measure of control.

Fatal Illnesses: The Split Focus

Not all fatal illnesses are immediately debilitating. Your parent, though fatally ill, may still be in pretty good shape—lucid, able to talk, ambulatory, even able to travel. If this is the case, you and your family may have to live with two distinctly different perspectives for months or even years.

One part of your attention will be fixed on living, enjoying the moment, making plans, keeping busy. Yet another part will dwell on dying, and all the fears that raises. There will be a shifting back and forth.

My father had tearful conversations with friends and relatives. He would often get upset, perhaps because he knew that the conversation could be his very last with them.

But he was also very much focused on living. He went out to dinner with relatives, enjoyed the meals my mother prepared, and kept hoping that he would have a couple more years. Every now and again, the other focus would emerge. On the phone once he told me that he was postponing having a crown put on one of his teeth. It was going to cost a lot, and he didn't want to spend the money if he only had a little time to live. It was one of the few times when he revealed, although in a joking manner, that he was conscious of the imminence of his death.

Facing a fatal diagnosis does not mean giving up hope. It only means not postponing whatever needs to be taken care of.

People sometimes have surprising recoveries or live much longer than anyone expected. If you do all you can in expectation of your parent's death—deal with legal and financial concerns, have conversations about your relationship, feel and express your love, and say good-bye—then you can focus on helping everyone enjoy, in whatever ways possible, the last days, months, or even years together.

Gathering Information and Educating Yourself

Once your parent is given a serious or terminal diagnosis, you suddenly need to become an expert in areas you may know nothing about. Research you parent's diagnosis. It will help to know as much as you can about the prognosis and course of treatment. You may also be surprised at how much a layperson can learn in just a couple of hours. You won't be able to perform an operation, but the process of your parent's medical treatment—and the doctor's language for discussing it—may suddenly be demystified. Arm yourself with a notepad and pencil before setting about your research.

- Buy a pocket-sized medical dictionary.

- Go to the public library and consult or check out the most current lay medical books. Ask the reference librarian for help in finding the books most relevant to your parent's illness, and the ones that are most up to date.

- Ask the doctor or hospital for pamphlets. You can also ask for the name of the medical journal or journals that would be most likely to have articles on the treatment or pathology of your parent's illness. These journals will be available for consultation in the hospital library. Ask the reference librarian for help.

- Talk with your parent's doctor (get your parent's verbal or written permission first).

- Consult medical textbooks in the hospital library (choose books that are clinically oriented—again, the reference librarian can help you). Use the index to find the relevant sections, and have your medical dictionary with you.

Medical school libraries are another good resource for information. So are national research organizations, such as the American Cancer Society and the National Institutes of Health. The reference librarian in your public library can help get you phone numbers and addresses for these and other organizations.

Some of the books that I found particularly helpful are listed in the reference section at the end of this chapter.

Without some familiarity with medical language, you will feel completely at sea. You'll be trying to communicate in the world of doctors, nurses, and hospitals without speaking the language.

It would help if Berlitz had a tape called "Medical Language Made Easy." As none exists, you can request that health-care professionals speak to you in common, everyday English. Feel free to say, "I want to make sure I understand what you're telling me. I'm going to try to explain it to you as I understand it. Please tell me if I have it right."

Catherine recalls the doctor coming in and saying in front of her parents, "There is tumor tissue and we're calling in the oncologist." Her parents didn't realize that the doctor had said that Catherine's mother had cancer. Catherine had to serve as translator.

References

These are some of the books that I found particularly helpful:

Dorland, W.A. (1988) *Dorland's Illustrated Medical Dictionary*, 27th ed. Philadelphia: Saunders.

Melloni, J. (1985) *Melloni's Illustrated Medical Dictionary*, 2nd ed. Baltimore: Williams and Wilkins.

Schroeder, S.A. (1992) *Current Medical Diagnosis and Treatment*, 31st ed. Norwalk, CN: Appleton and Lange.

(1990) *Handbook of Non-prescription Drugs*. 9th ed. Washington, D.C.: American Pharmaceutical Association.

(1992) P.D.R. *The Physician's Desk Reference*, 46th ed. Montvale, NJ: Medical Economics Data.

Marcy's Story

Marcy recently graduated from Michigan State University College of Osteopathic Medicine and is currently working as an intern. Her father worked as a tailor and men's clothing salesman in Flint, Michigan. Marcy was 33 when he died.

He was a loving father, but he wasn't very demonstrative; he and Marcy had a close but restrained relationship. He had grown up in Poland, fleeing when the Nazis invaded. Marcy had heard friends of her father who knew him before the war describe him as open and kind—the sort of person who would light up a room when he walked in. Marcy knew him as reserved, tired, and preoccupied, but occasionally caught glimpses of his younger self. He still retained a wonderful sense of humor; and at the parties they attended as a family, he would always sing along with the accordion player.

"The man I knew was serious, quiet, his mind in other places. I remember how he made me breakfast before school—soft-boiled eggs and toast in our Midwestern kitchen. He gave me a deep love of music, art, and flowers. I grew up with the most beautiful lawn in the neighborhood and roses beneath my window. I remember him working in the yard in his undershirt, relaxing. He spoke six languages.

"I know only glimpses of his burdens and of the small rooms where he lived with his family—of the Warsaw streets, the chocolate factory where he worked; how his father polished the family's shoes on Sunday. I know that one day he and his sister exited the train at night on the opposite side of the platform when they saw German soldiers. They walked until they were certain they were in Russia.

"My father ended up in a nursing home, much to our horror. He had a stroke when he was 59. He lived with my mother in their home for 10 years after that; but then he became debilitated, more and more withdrawn. When he fell and broke his hip, that was the beginning of the end. That happened about a year and half before he died. His leg was amputated. There was no coming back. And about six months before he died, he developed a problem with choking when he ate, so eating became very difficult. By the time he died, he weighed only 80 pounds.

"I visited him regularly. I don't remember how many times I'd walk out of that nursing home crying because he was in such bad shape.

"One Sunday night when I came home from work, my mother called to tell me that his blood pressure had dropped and he was having a hard time breathing. I got into the car and drove to the nursing home; and the next day, we called my brother to come home from Salt Lake City. The three of us started a round-the-clock vigil that lasted a week.

"He had the first room at the end of the hall. Every night we would push his bed down to the lounge. There were couches in the lounge and a huge pillow you could lie on. You could sleep there and be comfortable.

"We had a really hard time, because he didn't have any medical intervention—no pain medication, no I.V.'s. It was a choice we'd made, and it was a hard one. We knew if we took him to the hospital, he would probably get more intervention than we could handle; they might try to prolong his life with blood pressure elevators and I.V. fluids.

"In hindsight, I'm sorry that we couldn't at least have had an I.V. to keep him from getting dehydrated.

"The rabbi helped us stay in touch with the fact that death is a normal process. We live in a society that doesn't really accept that. So my father had, in a way, a very unadulterated death. We watched him die the way people all over the world die.

"It seemed to go on forever. He was breathing 60 times a minute through his mouth. It was really hard to watch. All we could do was be there with him. You can read about these breathing patterns; but until you see it, it's really strange.

"There had been so much loss of dignity in the way he was, as a stroke patient, and then as a nursing home patient. He was incontinent, and couldn't feed himself. But there was something about the last days of his dying, a kind of grace and dignity that hadn't been there before. For the first few days, he could squeeze our hands, and he could kiss our hands if we put them to his mouth, or he could kiss our cheek if we bent down; and then he wasn't able to do that either.

"We kept wondering when it would be. Finally, on Saturday night, I noticed his skin looked more and more discolored and his arms and legs were really cold because his circulation was starting to fail. And when the nurse came, she shut the doors and pulled the curtains, which she hadn't done before, and she said it would probably be tonight. Shortly after, his breathing changed. It had been rapid and now it was erratic. He died in about 10 minutes. As he took his last gasp, he kind of opened his eyes, and squinted like he was looking hard at something and then his breath stopped and he was gone. I remember saying, 'Oh, Dad, did you really die?' I just couldn't believe it. Then I just collapsed. I was hysterical even though I had known it was going to happen. He died in my arms.

"I wanted to capture the intimacy of those last moments, so I took pictures. I wanted to have a visual record of my father's body. My most precious photo is the one taken right before he died, when his eyes were still open. It took me about six months to take the film in. But I was surprised when I got the film back to see it wasn't as bad as I thought to have those photos. In fact, I was glad.

"Then we sat with him for about two hours. I had this idea, I don't know where I got it, but I wanted to wash his body. I had given him many baths during this time, and had really taken good care of him. I would clean him, turn him, rub him with cream.

"So when he died I wanted to wash him. It wasn't like he needed to be cleaned up, but it was just a way for us, for me, to say good-bye to his body, because I had come to know it so well—every muscle, every bone, and his face and ears and everything. So we got some water and washed him. My brother helped, even though he had never bathed him before. And my mother watched.

"One of the things that really struck me the whole time he was dying was that it was such a privilege to be with him for his death. He had lived in a war-torn situation—both his parents died during the war. It was a privilege to live in relative peacetime and to be able to be there with him when he died.

"We not only had the grief of his death, but we had the grief of his life and what had happened to him. So many losses. First, he lost his family in Poland. Then he had a small business, working on alterations in a musty cavernous basement, a trade he apprenticed for at age 12. After 10 years, the business folded. He had the stroke and lost his leg when he was only 59. We'd had years of being sad about everything that had happened to him; but, finally, we could put it all together. We could grieve for the loss of his life as well as for the losses he suffered during his lifetime."

3

The Intimate Details
of Death

We are side by side. I am lying on the couch in the living room next to my father, who is lying on his hospital bed. We are watching T.V. My mother is asleep in the bedroom. He wants to watch the news; I want to watch a murder mystery. My father is dying, and I should be sensitive to his wishes. But I am drained and tired and need to unwind. It is clear that we should watch what he wants; but I want to watch what I want.

Since he drifts in and out, when I notice that he has fallen asleep, I change the channel. At one point, he awakens and asks, "What junk are you watching?" Those are to be his last words.

When your parent is dying, the last hours, days, and weeks, will be filled with funny, grim, embarrassing, tiring, and emotional moments. You may have to cope with incontinence, decisions about I.V.'s and respirators, and a lot of confused feelings.

It is very easy in such circumstances to become frightened and overwhelmed. You want to do the right thing, but you don't always know what that would be.

In the same way in which a prepared childbirth class helps you get ready for birth, this chapter will help you prepare for death. You will learn what to expect, what you might see, what you can do, what your choices are, and how to handle what is going on, both in terms of your parent and yourself. If you are educated about death, and not afraid, you can be much more flexible, present, and responsive when the pressure is on.

Preparing is not like rehearsing for a performance. There is no right way to do what needs to be done. But there are three guiding principles that you may find useful:

- When your parent is dying, be there as much as you can.

- Respect your parent's wishes.

- Maximize human, noninstitutional contact.

If the decision is left up to you, make a conscious choice about where your parent will die. This is very difficult, because it involves admitting that your parent *will* die. It also necessitates talking to your parent about this stark reality.

How can people talk to their parents about dying without scaring them? One way to broach the subject is to discuss it in terms of contingency plans: "In the worst-case scenario, Mom, if you don't get better, where would you like to be? What would you like us to arrange?" Or, "I'd like to feel as much as possible that I'm carrying out your wishes. So if things get to the point where a decision has to be made, where do you think you'd feel most comfortable?"

As you read the sections that follow, remember that where the death takes place is not as important as your parent being surrounded by people who are known and loved: who will be prepared to accept your parent's dying and can help rather than hinder death's natural progress.

The Pros and Cons of Hospitals and Nursing Homes Versus a Home Death

Knowing Your Options

Your parents' health insurance will be one of the prime determinants in their choice of institutional care. Your mother or father's diagnosis will be the second factor. In 1983, Medicare began to pay hospitals based on diagnostic related groupings (DRGs). This means that the hospital is paid a fixed rate for each admission, according to the diagnosis. The diagnosis then determines length of the hospital stay.

Becky recalls:

> I couldn't believe they were going to kick my father out of the hospital. He was hooked up to every tube imaginable; he was practically in a coma. And they're telling us they're going to discharge him; they can't keep him. This is when I found out about hospital DRGs: they couldn't keep him any longer, based on his diagnosis. He either had to go into home health care or a nursing home. I was completely shocked. I just assumed he would stay in the hospital the whole time.
>
> What had been really difficult now became a nightmare. We didn't know what to do. We went to see the social worker, feeling pretty desperate. She mentioned a third choice, hospice, for the first time. But my mother didn't want to hear about it: hospice was for people who are dying. She decided she

would put my father in a nursing home instead. She would go and stay with him every day, but not have to care for him at night.

But nursing home care was going to cost $3500 a month. Our insurance wouldn't pay very much of that. Medicare would only pay for four or five days. My mother decided to use her savings. Her idea was that she would keep my father in a nursing home for a few weeks until she could get organized, and then she would bring him home. But when we went to visit the nursing home, she changed her mind. She couldn't deal with leaving him there.

There are many different types of nursing homes, with different levels of service. When your parent becomes terminally ill, he or she will most likely end up in an intermediate care facility, or skilled nursing home, where 24-hour care is given and there is a high level of medical service available.

A hospital or nursing home can be a good choice if your parent does not want you to care for him or her by yourself, if your schedule or other obligations will not allow it and other family support is unavailable, or if your parent's pain and symptoms are only controllable in a hospital or skilled nursing facility. In an institutional setting, your parent will be surrounded by people who are experienced in handling illness. Both hospitals and nursing homes have medication and high-tech equipment on hand. For instance, the use of I.V.'s and respirators can in some cases make your parent's last hours or days more comfortable.

In a hospital or nursing home, if your parent is incontinent or unconscious for long periods of time, you will not be overburdened by the responsibility of round-the-clock care. You can visit, spend time, help, and go home and get a good night's rest. If you feel guilty leaving your parent, examine your options. But don't be pressured by guilt into something you can't handle.

Sometimes, there is too much intervention, especially in hospitals. Some of the equipment, such as respirators, can hurt as much as help (a tube is placed in the patient's throat to deliver air, but he or she cannot talk or eat, and needs to be fed intravenously).

In hospitals and nursing homes, the standard of good care is based only on visible tasks and services. Often nurses and aides are treated like factory workers on an assembly line. Were the medications given on time? How many I.V.'s were hooked up, how many temperatures taken, how many wet beds changed? They are not asked to record, nor are they judged by, how many hands they held, how many words of comfort they offered, how many family members they helped.

And yet, extraordinary compassion can be found in such places, too. Becky tells this story about her father's last days in the hospital:

> *The swelling in his arm was so bad that they told him they were going to have to bring somebody in to cut his wedding ring off. That was the first time I had ever seen him upset. He wasn't going to let them do it. My mother was also very upset. And then this wonderful nurse's aide came in. I don't know what she put on, Vaseline or something, but she kept working on it until it came off. The doctors had figured they would just cut it off. But this nurse's aide recognized that both of my parents would go to pieces over this. It was a little thing, but it was so symbolic of the real loss they were facing.*

How You Can Help, Even in a Hospital Setting

There definitely are some things you can do that will improve your parent's time in the hospital. When possible, visit daily. As your parent gets closer to death, try to make sure that a family member or close friend is present at all times. Near the end, most hospitals will allow you or another relation to spend the night in your parent's room.

There is usually one doctor in charge. Make sure that you know the doctor and that the doctor knows you. Also make an appointment to speak with the social worker assigned to your parent's ward. Social workers usually are good sources of information and moral support.

Develop a relationship with the nurses on the ward. Get to know their names and try to keep track of their work assignments (who's on the night shift, who works during the day?). If you need to talk to one of the nurses, try to do so at a time that's mutually convenient for you. Remain sensitive to the fact that your parent is just one of many individuals under a given nurse's care.

What You Should Know About Life Support

It is very important to discuss in advance what, if any, heroic efforts your parent would choose if a medical crisis threatens imminent death. There are three types of life support procedures most commonly used in hospitals and skilled nursing facilities:

Resuscitation. Cardiopulmonary Resuscitation (CPR) includes mouth-to-mouth resuscitation, external chest compression, electric shock to restart the heart, insertion of a tube to open air passageways, injection of medication into the heart, or open-chest heart massage.

Mechanical breathing. A machine called a respirator or ventilator forces air into the lungs and maintains respiration artificially.

Artificial nutrition and hydration. This entails using an I.V. or more invasive procedures, including feeding through a nasogastric tube (inserted through a nostril into the stomach), a tube inserted into the stomach directly (gastrostomy), or in the upper end of the small intestine (jejunostomy) when a person is in a coma or otherwise unable to be fed any other way. ·

People should ask their parents explicitly:

- Do they want to be placed on machinery if some of their bodily functions fail?

- Do they want every effort to be made to revive them if their heart stops working? In hospitals this distinction is known as code versus no code or DNR (do not revive). Your parent's chart will be marked code or no code, according to his or her instructions.

Decisions regarding code or no code, medication, chemotherapy, and the use of respirators are very difficult to make. When possible, arrange for your parent to discuss these issues with friends, family members, nurses and doctors, and/or a medical social worker before making the commitment to a particular course. If your parent is not in a position to decide, avail yourself of the same resources: these are not decisions to be made casually.

The Option of Home Death

If it is possible, I would recommend finding a way to help your parents die either in your home or theirs. Here they will be in familiar surroundings, with their family, and exercising more control over their care.

The big question is whether you feel that you could handle taking care of your parent if this choice is made. Keep in mind that there are several routes to follow with a home death depending on your individual resources (both financial and emotional). You and other family members can be the primary caregivers; you can hire someone else to be the primary caregiver; or you can hire someone to assist you part-time (usually a nurse or nurse's aide).

The first option will tax all your physical and emotional resources; the second and third options can be enormously draining financially. But some people would no sooner think of ducking these challenges than they would of farming their children out to boarding schools, say, during pottie-training or the difficult years of adolescence. Such intense feelings of family loyalty are not something that can be mandated, here or anywhere else. Depending on your background and circumstances, you either feel them or you don't. If you *are* someone who would like to consider a home death for your parent, these are some of the questions you'll first need to answer.

1. Analyze your particular situation: What are your present responsibilities at work and at home? Is it feasible for you to take enough time off? How long could you manage being with your parent, either in their home or your home? What's the timeframe you will be dealing with? Hospice requires a six-month prognosis for someone to be accepted into their program.

2. How many family members or friends are available to share the responsibility of your parent's care? How many shifts would you yourself have to take? Can you afford to hire help? If you do plan to hire help, look for an accredited or licensed home health care agency. A useful resource is *A Consumer Guide to Home Health Care*, updated in 1991. You can order this booklet for $4.00 from the National Consumers League, 815 15th Street NW, Suite 516, Washington, D.C. 20005; phone (202) 639-8140.

3. Do you feel capable of handling the physical problems presented by your parent's illness? You might have to

- Give your mom or dad a bed bath
- Help your parent use a bedpan

- Change a bed while your parent is in it

- Transfer your parent from bed to chair and back again

- Deal with nausea, loss of appetite, and constipation

- Clean up vomit, urine, and diarrhea

- Learn how to use oxygen equipment

- Field your children's questions and involve them in your parent's care

When you are closely involved with a dying parent, there are bound to be some difficult and embarrassing moments.

One friend recalls the first time she took her mother to the bathroom and saw that she had messed her pants. "I was just kind of mortified. I thought, how am I going to do this? And then I thought, 'She did you.' So I just did it."

So many people I talked with discovered that they could just do it. I remember my own surprise at what I could manage. Putting my father's penis over the edge of a bucket to help him urinate, handling my father's parts: things that were unimaginable as we were, but perfectly natural in our present situation.

Becky and her mother and sister tried to get her father into the bathroom every time he had to use it. That involved getting him out of bed.

> It was quite wild—at one point he fell on the floor. It was really hard physically, because he didn't have any strength. After a couple of days, we finally decided it would be better to use diapers. It was a strange feeling to be caring for your parent like an infant. But they brought you into the world and did that for you, and now you are helping them go out of the world and doing it for them.

A client recalls noticing that her father had wet himself. "I didn't want to make him feel uncomfortable, so I asked if he wanted me to give him a washcloth so he could clean himself up. He just lay back and said, no, that's okay—you go ahead and do it."

Initially, it may feel totally inappropriate to see your parent so exposed. But what may be akward at first becomes easier over time.

One client told me:

> *I brought my mother home, and instantaneous-*
> *ly I became a full-time loving daughter and nurse. I*
> *was a little overwhelmed with the idea of being over-*
> *whelmed. I wondered whether I had it in me to drop*
> *everything and stay by her side 24 hours a day*
> *without losing my mind. It's not been easy. It's*
> *probably the most difficult thing I've ever done. I've*
> *been lucky. I have a superior support system. I have*
> *friends that help day or night. I have a daughter*
> *who does as much as she can. I have a great boss,*
> *and no young children at home. I'm happier each*
> *day that I'm able to do this for her.*

In the past, when I had allowed the thought of my father's death to enter my mind, I always hoped he would die at home. I knew how much he hated hospitals. Intellectually, I thought that a home death was a great idea; but emotionally I was petrified when the possibility became a reality. I had no idea of what to do, how to act, what I would see, how I would handle it. I feared that if my father were to have another seizure, I would rush him as quickly as possible to a hospital to let *them* deal with his death. I was terrified at the idea of *seeing* my father die.

If you are considering a home death, the key resource to rely on will be the hospice program.

Hospice—An Invaluable Resource

To be accepted in a hospice program, your parent must be terminally ill, with a life expectancy of six months; be willing to receive care at home; and have a primary caretaker available. Both Medicaid and Medicare cover hospice services.

Hospice helps with death in the way that midwives help with birth. No one would suggest a home birth without the assistance of professionals. If you choose a home death for your parent, it is essential that you contact hospice.

You can find the hospice service agency in your area through hospitals and doctors or in the phone book under "hospice." *Hospice Link* is a referral service that gives information about hospice care and can tell you about programs in your area. Their number is 1-800-331-1620.

Hospice has a very clear philosophy that translates into the kind of real support you'll need. They want patients to live until they die; they want patients' families to live with them as they are dying, and to go on living afterwards.

Although hospice is relatively new in this country, there is now a national organization in place with over 1700 programs.

Jane Loubert, a hospice nurse, describes what she considers to be the most important aspects of the program:

> *Hospice is a place where you allow people choices. You educate them, let them do what feels right, and give them some control. Also, it's a great deal for people's Medicare monies. You get an enormous amount of services: nurses, volunteers, physicians, pastoral care, medication, home health care (up to 20 hours per week), durable medical equipment (like hospital beds)—for up to seven months. If you choose hospice, you are not turning your back on traditional medicine, which may have given all it could. Now you just may need another kind of help.*

Becky recalls:

> *I don't know what would have happened to us*
> *if it weren't for hospice. That program really saved*
> *us. They brought us bed equipment, a portable*
> *toilet, a urinal—everything we would need to take*
> *care of my father as though he were in the hospital,*
> *except we're the ones providing all the care. The*
> *nurse became the manager of our case. She sat for*
> *hours talking with my mother and sister. I wasn't*
> *there but they told me all about it. It's so helpful*
> *just to have them talk about dying with you. They*
> *do it on every level—the physical, what happens to*
> *the body; and the emotional, the loss you're going to*
> *have. She even briefed them about how his death*
> *might occur, that the clotting factor might go and*
> *he would hemorrhage and die quickly but be covered*
> *with blood. She trained them how to cope with that.*
> *Can you imagine this happening and not knowing*
> *what to do? She told them it was important to get*
> *dark towels and put them around and let the blood*
> *go into the towels. And to make sure they didn't*
> *panic. It would be a very fast way to go, but it*
> *would be shocking if you didn't expect it, because of*
> *all the blood. Some might even come out of his*
> *mouth. They knew it would be difficult, but my*
> *mother and sister actually felt prepared.*

One man told me, "You could count on their help day or
night. One evening my mother was in a lot of pain and the
nurse came out to our house at 11:30 p.m. in order to give her
some medication."

I remember my first contact with hospice. The social
worker had come to visit and was talking to my father, explain-
ing why she was there and how she could help. She noticed, as
she talked, that both he and the bed needed to be cleaned up.
But I was surprised when she asked for a washcloth. She was

very dressed up. Gently, talking all the while, she washed him, then called me over to show me how to change his bed. I, too, am a social worker. But I have never cleaned anybody up. She was crossing some border I had been taught to observe, making it natural and professional to connect with a person in a very intimate way.

Hospice staff never have an "Oh well, that's just what happens with this illness" attitude. They look at each symptom as a disease in itself to be diagnosed and treated. And they are always aggressive in how they manage pain. Their goal is to have pain controlled as soon as possible, including the pain that comes from fear, anxiety, and depression.

But what makes hospice so special and so helpful is that they are also geared to helping *you*. Traditional medical staff may have appeared bothered by your questions and concerns. They are there to treat your parent, not you. But hospice is another story, and a better one. They consider helping you to be part of their work. Your entire family will receive loving attention. Medicaid and Medicare benefits cover hospice care. No one is turned away for lack of money.

One night the hospice nurse came by at 6:00 p.m. After looking in at my father, she stayed on. She could sense that I needed support. So she sat around the dining room table listening to me talk. I felt scared, yet unable to tell her that. But just her presence was a comfort. I kept asking her how much longer she thought it would be; it was strange. But I had to start making plans, since I could only be away from home a few weeks. If it was a few months before my father died, I would have had to make other arrangements.

People are often surprised at the range of help hospice is willing to give. Besides providing a nurse, hospice also arranged for volunteers to spell Toby's sister, Lisa, so that she could get out of the house. His mother had been writing a book, but could no longer work on it. One of the volunteers actually took home the chapters and retyped them. "They did whatever was needed."

Hospice provides a strong and sensitive support system that exists round the clock. If a tube falls out at 3:00 a.m. and you're having trouble trying to replace it, you have someone to call.

In my own experience, I found hospice to be a never-ending source of ideas. Their vision of good care ranges from practical to emotional considerations, from wet beds to lonely moments to the intense feelings of frustration that can overcome caregivers and their charges.

My friend Cathy recalls:

> So there we are at home. By this time my mother is incontinent. She's wetting herself. And the bed's wet. There's a cross-sheet we've got to get off, but we don't know how to move my mother. My brother and I have no idea what to do. She's a dead weight by now. We're trying to get this wet sheet off, and she's so embarrassed. "I'm so nasty and dirty," she says. We say, "It's fine. You're doing so well."
>
> I looked at my brother and pretended I was about to perform the tablecloth trick—you know, where those cartoon characters are able to pull a tablecloth off without disturbing the glasses sitting on top of it.

A nurse's aide from hospice taught Cathy and her brother how to use a cross-sheet. This is the sheet you put across the bed, horizontally so it can be used as a pull-sheet to help you move a person in bed (so that the patient can be washed or changed and bed linens replaced).

If it's your dad you're taking care of, hospice will also teach you about condom catheters, a rubber condom with a tube at the tip that's connected to a urine collection bag. They'll also tell you where to buy adult diapers, and why plastic bedpans are better than metal ones (they don't feel as cold).

At the end, hospice will help you confirm that death has occurred, and will handle calls to the mortuary and your doctor.

Not all hospice agencies are the same. Some may have staff who work all night. Others are on call. Get accurate information ahead of time, so you know exactly what sort of help will be available. You might want to ask:

- Will your parent have to switch doctors in order to participate in the hospice program? (If the doctor is not affiliated with hospice, your parent can continue seeing him or her, but will be assigned a hospice doctor as well.)

- How available will the staff be? Will they be able to respond to an emergency in the middle of the night with a phone call or a visit?

- Do they have an inpatient facility available if things get too hard at home? How long can your parent remain in that facility? If there's not an inpatient facility, does the hospice organization have respite care (this is a place where your parent can stay for five days while family members recover and rest)?

Hospice is a great support system. And yet people sometimes find it difficult to contact hospice because it is so explicitly a program for the dying. This can be a very difficult emotional hurdle, both for patients and family members. One requirement for hospice participation is a doctor's statement that the patient will die within six months. Until your parent becomes bedridden, or unless you've experienced the tension of medical emergencies, hospice can seem like too drastic a step.

Other people—even those who are already very sick— avoid contacting hospice because they don't want strangers coming into their home, or they don't want their children to see them as dying or to burden them with their care.

Many people misjudge the support they'll need. When Fred's father was sent home from the hospital it was clear that he would simply die in his sleep in a few days. But Fred's mother, who was 80, couldn't really handle the strain. Other family members had arranged for a housekeeper, and visited frequently. But Fred's mother was afraid to be alone when the death occurred and his father ended up back in the hospital. Hospice support might have meant that he could have died at home.

When Death Is Imminent

Whether your parent is dying at home or in the hospital, the most important advice I can share is that your presence matters. It is not necessarily what you do or say; it's just being there.

My friend Kim recalls:

> *My mother and I were in my father's hospital room. He was unconscious, having a tremendous amount of trouble breathing, and obviously dying. We had all agreed not to ask for respirators or extraordinary measures. I had it in my mind he was going to die then, and we weren't going to do anything to prolong his life. At the same time, my mind didn't understand that. I rushed into the hall to call a doctor, only half realizing there was nothing the doctor could do. Anyway, he didn't come. Fifteen minutes later, a young resident appeared. He sat and listened to my father's breathing and told us he was very critical. I kept wishing somebody could do something despite our decision. But all we could do was hold my father as he stopped breathing.*

Kim may have felt confused and anxious, but he still managed to be there. And even though all he could do was hold his father as he stopped breathing, Kim's very presence was a comfort.

If you are not able to be with your parent every day (because of long distance or the demands of work or home), keep in contact with those who are there. Make it clear that you want to know what is really happening. Sometimes family members, thinking they are being kind, protect and misinform those who are present.

Tell your family that you don't want information withheld, and that, if possible, you would like to be there when death is imminent.

If your parent is in a hospital or nursing home, a close and good connection with the staff can make a difference. If they keep in touch and alert you to serious changes, it is more likely that you can be present at the moment when your parent dies, even if you live far away.

Kathryn's experience is a good example. She is a contract negotiator who lives in New York City. Her mother was in a hospital in Cokato, Minnesota. Kathryn wanted to be with her mother when she died, and had let the hospital staff know. They were cooperative, and remained sensitive to the fact that she lived so far away. They involved her, long distance, in all the decisions that had to be made.

When her mother started to go downhill, Kathryn was in the middle of labor negotiations and couldn't leave town very easily. But the doctor and nurses kept in touch by phone.

One night a nurse called and told me my mother was failing and I better come soon. She might die within 24 hours. I told her to tell my mother to hold on till I got there. Then I drove like a maniac to the airport, rushed to the hospital, and literally ran into her room shouting, "It's Kathryn and I'm here and I'm not going to leave." I kept repeating that over and over again. I remember apologizing for being so redundant. I just wanted her to know I was there. I took her hand and she moved her eyes. I'm sure she knew it was me.

The hospital let me sleep on the next bed and gave me blankets and pillows. They were fabulous. The nurse in charge would bring snacks and coffee to me. I was there holding my mother when she drew her last breath.

Sometimes nobody can predict what will happen. And if you and your parent live far away from each other it can be hard to travel back and forth without a definite timeframe.

Susan, for example, lived in Georgia; her father was in Florida. When he became ill, Susan began to travel back and forth between the two states. Unlike Kathryn's situation, where the medical staff were able to recognize that her mother was dying, Susan's father kept taking a turn for the worse and then getting better. The medical staff told her that it would be a long haul. But it turned out that the one turn for the worse she didn't respond to was the one when her father died. She felt terrible— for her father, who was alone when he died; and for herself. But she hadn't done anything wrong. She had two young children and a full-time job. How many trips could she make from Georgia to Florida and back again? Was there a right number? Five? Twenty-five?

Although Susan wasn't able to be with her father when he died, she *had* been present when her mother died. She learned something important from both experiences. "There is no right or wrong. What's most important is knowing you've done the best you can."

Becky figures that she made about eight or nine trips from New York City to Florida in January and February, when her father became ill. Her description of her last commute home reflects the impossible situation one is faced with when your home and job are in one place, and your parent is in another.

I really didn't want to go back to New York City, but I had a class to teach the next day. When I got to the airport, they didn't have a ticket for me.

*I should have known then—it was a sign I
shouldn't go; but then they found a first-class seat
for me and I took it.*

*The fare was $322, when usually it is only
$99. When I got to the gate, the plane was over-
booked. They asked people to give up their seats if
too many people showed up. I volunteered. As I was
sitting there, I went from wanting the ticket to not
wanting it. I felt some incredible pull to stay. Finally they announced that we could all board. I ended
up in this horrible seat, in the smoking section.
Once on the plane, I couldn't believe I was leaving.
I just knew I shouldn't go. But I did. There was
just no way to know what was going to happen. I
would have to continue to go back and forth, back
and forth.*

*That was Sunday. My father died two days
later. I wasn't there.*

If you can't be *present*, be a *presence*. My cousin, who lives
in New Jersey, had just returned home from Florida, where he
had been visiting his sick father, when his mother and brother
phoned at midnight. His father was back in the hospital; he was
dying. My cousin got on the phone, and my aunt held it to my
uncle's ear. Even though my uncle couldn't speak, he could still
hear. My cousin said good-bye and spoke words of love; the
phone call ended. My uncle took two more breaths and then
died.

Being there as much as you can, for as long as you can,
will help both you and your parent. But it's important to
remember that this isn't a situation within your control. Death
doesn't follow any schedules.

Don't leave everything important you want to say for the
very last moments. Even if it means repeating yourself, say what
you need to throughout your parent's illness. In that way, you
can be closely connected to your mom or dad even if you are

absent at the moment of death. It *is* important that *someone* from the family (or a close friend) be present, so that your parent is not alone.

Know What To Expect

It helps you cope if you know what happens at death. Although some people simply lie down, close their eyes, stop breathing, and die very peacefully, many spend their last day or hours making sounds and presenting sights that can be very distressing to those looking on. These can include changes in color and body temperature, gasping for breath, or breathing very rapidly or very wetly, as if drowning. The cessation of breath itself can be traumatic. My cousin Joan remembers, "I was feeling very centered and comforted by my Uncle Sid's breath when I was with him. Then I realized that he was going to *stop* breathing. Dying seemed okay, but not breathing was hard to take."

When you know what signs and symbols are part of the normal process of dying—and in which situations intervention is impossible, it becomes easier to manage your emotions. Hospice publishes a list of common symptoms and how to handle them.

1. The arms and legs of your parent's body may become cool to the touch, and you may notice the underside of their body becoming much darker in color. These symptoms are a result of blood circulation slowing down. Keep warm blankets on the patient (but not electric ones) to prevent him/her from becoming overly cold.

2. Your parent will gradually spend more and more time sleeping, and at times may be difficult to arouse. This is a result of a change in the body's metabolism. Plan to spend more time together during those times when he/she is most alert.

3. Mental clarity may vary. Your parent may become increasingly confused about time, place, and the identity of close and familiar people. Again, this is a result of metabolic changes. Coma may occur. Remind your parent about what day it is, what time it is, and who is in the room.

4. Loss of control of urine and bowel movements (incontinence) is often not a problem until death becomes imminent. You can buy absorbent pads to place under your parent for comfort and cleanliness, or the doctor can order a catheter.

5. Oral secretions may become more profuse and collect in the back of the throat. You may have heard this referred to as the "death rattle." This symptom results from a decrease in the body's intake of fluids, and inability to cough up normal saliva. Elevating the head of the bed with pillows (or obtaining a hospital bed) will make breathing easier. Swabbing the mouth and lips with lemon-glycerine swabs also gives comfort. Ice chips, drinks with a straw, and a cool moist washcloth will relieve feelings of dehydration. A cool-mist humidifier to increase the humidity in the room will also help.

6. Clarity of hearing and vision may decrease. You may want to keep lights on in the room when vision decreases. *Never* assume that your parent cannot hear you, as hearing is the last of the five senses to be lost.

7. You may notice your parent becoming restless, pulling at the bed linen, and having visions of people or things that do not exist. These symptoms are a result of a decrease in oxygen circulation to the brain and a change in the body's metabolism. Talk calmly to your parent so as not to startle or frighten your parent further.

8. Your parent will have decreased need for food and drink, because the body will naturally begin to conserve energy which is expended on these tasks. A nurse or doctor can give you information on food which may be helpful in maintaining nutritional status.

9. While your parent is sleeping, you may notice a change to irregular breathing patterns that include 10–30-second periods of no breathing. The medical term for this is apnea. It's very common and indicative of a decrease in circulation and buildup in the body's waste products. Elevating the head of the bed sometimes makes breathing more regular.

10. You will notice that the amount of urine will decrease as death comes closer. If there is a bladder catheter in place, there may be a need to irrigate it in order to prevent blockage.

This will be a time of many painful moments. It hurts to see your parent so dependent; and your parent will be having such a hard time. Many people seem to be very afraid in their last days and hours, contending with the fear of dying, fear of the unknown, fear that the process of death will be painful, and fear of their own loss of control.

If you understand how vulnerable and afraid your parent feels, it will become easier to handle his or her behavior. My father started banging his fist against the side of his bed to get our attention when he could have simply waved, as we were in the same room. A neighbor's mother would wake her three or four times a night to change her slightly damp diaper. Demanding and self-centered behavior is not uncommon. Respond with kindness whenever you can.

Illness and fear can make people so enormously hostile, cantankerous, paranoid, and blaming that caring for them seems like a thankless task. You may find yourself actually wanting to hit your mother or scream "shut up!" at your father.

If this is the case, quickly find someone you can talk with. Describe what's going on. You need a steady source of support in this kind of situation. If an understanding friend or family member isn't at hand, see a professional. Don't refrain from making jokes when you describe how horribly your parent has behaved—laughing about the situation is one way to release tension.

You also need to schedule enough breaks for yourself so that you don't go crazy, too. Get other family members, or professional caretakers, to spell you. Hospice also has programs that afford time-outs for the primary caregiver.

Storybook-perfect deaths are the exception rather than the rule. Susan described her father's last day:

> *The day he died we were all there. He was hallucinating. He spent a lot of time thinking and worrying about money; it was one of his obsessions. At around 3:00 in the afternoon, he started saying, "You have to get your money out. The banks are closing. Get your money out before it's too late!" It's sort of comical to think about. His metaphor for death was the banks closing.*
>
> *Then later that night he was sitting in a chair. He was sitting up. It was amazing. He was very weak and about to die, but all of a sudden, he said, "Who's gonna do the funeral?" And so we told him and he said, "I want to take Communion." Now you have to understand, he was Jewish; but he had always had this conflict about being a Jew, and never believed in God. Now he's saying, "Give me the wafer." He put his hand out. This man never went to Mass; he wasn't Catholic. There wasn't a Catholic drop of blood in his body and he said,*

"Give me the wafer." I looked at my mother like, what's going on? And she said, "Give him the wafer." So I pretended to give him a wafer.

And he acted out Communion. He put the wafer in his mouth, the whole thing. As though Jesus Christ had come to him and he was being given the last rites. It was amazing. And when he was done, he handed the plate back, and then that was over. It was late at night and we left. We didn't think he was going to die that night, or we would have stayed.

It's difficult sometimes to gauge the proper decorum for your parent's death. One family I know whose father was dying gathered in his hospital room and literally tiptoed around, talking in a quiet and hushed manner. The nurse, on the other hand, was noisy and talkative. This annoyed them, until the nurse took them aside and told them, "You know, I think your father can hear you. Talk to him—this will be your last chance."

Deciding how best to help can also be hard. A friend of mine played music tapes of her father's favorite songs over and over again. When her father died, her brother said, "Well, Dad, at least you don't have to listen to those tapes anymore!" Suddenly, she wasn't sure that what she had done had been helpful at all. Her father had been unconscious and unable to make his wishes known.

Resign yourself now to the idea that you will make some mistakes of judgment and behavior. You're not a mind-reader; and you're treading in new territory. What's important is not that you do everything perfectly, but rather that you do your best. This is what will give you comfort in later years.

How To Know that Death Has Occurred

My friend Diane remembers asking a hospice nurse with some embarrassment, "How will I know when my aunt has died?"

These are the signs to look for:

- No breathing
- No heartbeat
- Loss of control of bowel or bladder
- No response to verbal commands or shaking
- Eyelids slightly open
- Eyes fixed on a certain spot
- Jaws relaxed and mouth slightly open

Know When To Let Go

As important as it is to hold someone close, it is also important to know when to let go.

Elizabeth, a social worker from Switzerland, had been very close to her father. She sat by his bedside as he was dying, and kept reaching out to hold his hand. But he kept pushing her away. She couldn't understand why. Later she realized that she had been begging him, over and over again, "Please don't die." He couldn't take her hand, because she was holding him back.

A client of mine had visited her father regularly; then she skipped one day, feeling tired and drained. The rest of her large family had been with him all day. But, shortly after they left, he died. My client felt guilty. A nun, who knew her father well, told her, "He needed that time alone so he could let go. Your father was a person very concerned with his family's feelings. It would have been hard for him to die with you present."

Everyone's parents are different. There is no one prescription for how to best help them.

My uncle told my aunt, "no hospice, no hospital bed, no porta johns" while their two sons were visiting. He didn't want any evidence around that he was clearly getting worse and dying. Even though both sons knew everything, he still wanted to put the best face on things. It made *him* feel better.

Then, when he was no longer able to eat or stand, my aunt asked him, "Do you want me to call hospice or the doctor?" He wanted the doctor. He was choosing to go to the hospital rather than to stay home. She knew he would be very upset if she called 911 for an ambulance, so she drove him to the hospital herself. She wasn't focusing on what *she* wanted or felt was best, but on what *he* wanted.

One client recalls feeling angry as she watched her mother try to kiss her father on the lips during a pause between breaths. "He was trying so hard to breathe, and each breath seemed like a struggle, I couldn't believe my mother was going to interfere with that process by kissing him. I wanted to yell, Take your hands off him!"

The main focus of everyone's concern should be the needs of the dying person—not your needs, not anyone else's. Your parent may try to keep going just for *you*. But when someone is fatally ill and in pain, hanging on like that can be an inhumane burden. Compassion must also sometimes include giving up and letting go.

When you find readiness to accept your parent's death, it will make death easier. Your mom or dad will no longer have to protect you or worry about how you are managing. They can focus on themselves. My friend Carol recalls telling her father that she wouldn't feel let down if he died. She remembers that he made a sound like "Whew," as if to say, "what a relief"—and died soon afterwards.

Rosa, an artist who lives in San Francisco, could see that her father was in terrible pain. Although only 65, he had suffered a severe heart attack.

> *I was alone in his hospital room with him, and*
> *I was breathing with him and telling him that it*
> *was okay for him to die. I felt him holding on, and*
> *realized he needed to know he had done everything*
> *he could and wouldn't be deserting us if he died. I*
> *recognized that he was trying to keep going for me*

*and my mother. I kept saying "It's okay. It's okay,"
and with that his breath eased and he let go. To me
that was the most beautiful and wondrous thing. I
was there holding his hand and helping him let go
of his breath.*

John's Story

John is a psychologist in a small town in Michigan. He's married, with two grown children, and has a younger brother. His father, a retired auto mechanic, was a very popular person and felt happy with his life. Unlike his son, however, he was not very introspective. This created some friction between them.

John's father was 79 years old when he died, after spending 28 days in the hospital. John was 45.

"My father had had a couple of heart attacks, so the thought of his dying was not far away. I became aware of many ambivalent feelings that earlier in my life I hadn't noticed. I had a very intense relationship with my father. There were aspects of him I genuinely appreciated, but I also had negative feelings toward him. It was hard for me to accept those. I had worshipped my father, but he was emotionally distant. He couldn't acknowledge his inner self and his feelings. I think I ended up feeling his disowned feelings—it was as if I became the opposite of my father.

"When my father was admitted to the hospital, the doctor told him that he had cancer of the pancreas, which was difficult to treat; but he never told him that it had spread extensively throughout his liver and lungs. My father wasn't feeling too bad, but wasn't able to keep any food down. I remember him asking if they did 'stomach transplants'—he felt if he could only eat, he'd feel okay.

"Then they started giving him chemotherapy. In 24 hours, he became disoriented, asking his best friend, "Who are you?" He thought the nurse was Jesus Christ, and tried to urinate in the bedpan even though he was wearing a chatheter. I learned from this experience to be very skeptical about the treatment doctors recommend to someone who is clearly dying.

"After the course of chemotherapy, it was quite apparent that he was failing badly. He couldn't even move his legs because he was so weak. I remember him asking, "Can you believe I'm going?" Despite that, right up until about the last week, he continued to have hope that something more positive lay ahead.

"My father had approached life with courage and humor. He approached his illness and death just like he had everything else. I remember when his sister started talking to him about heaven. She told him, 'When you get there, drop me a line.' He responded, 'You better lose some weight.'

"Shortly after chemotherapy, my father's veins became very weak and the nurse could no longer keep him on I.V.'s. They tried to put them in the hands, arms, feet, and legs—but they couldn't. So they wanted to stop the I.V.'s. But my father was very clear at this point. He didn't want to die. He wanted the doctor to start the I.V. And I didn't want him to have the additional misery of starvation on top of cancer. I said I wanted the doctor to start the I.V.'s.

"But the I.V. that they managed to get in his arm created so much pain, they had to take it out. The only other possibility was using the jugular in the neck. That sounded awful.

"An anesthesiologist was visiting the patient in the next bed, and had been called in because of his very great skill. Before he left, we asked him to do an I.V. on my father. And he did. He put it in the jugular, and it lasted two weeks. It saved my father from starvation.

"My wife and I spent every night with him. The night he died, I was with him at his bedside in the hospital, holding his hand. He had the interrupted breathing that occurs before death. He'd take a breath and then wouldn't breathe for 10 seconds, and then you'd think it was over and he would expel another breath.

"He was lying on his side and had this constant upflow from his stomach coming out of the side of his mouth, which I was suctioning out. The nurse came in and said she was going to turn him to make him more comfortable, but he was unconscious at this point, and I said to her, 'I don't think you should turn him, because he's got this constant drainage and it will choke him.' And she said, 'No, that's okay. I've got the suction, I'll handle it.' She turned him over, he immediately aspirated, became very red, was obviously struggling, and died. He choked and died.

"That bothered me. It disturbed me that we had done everything we could to make things right and at the very end it got messed up. We tried to handle things as he would have wanted. We knew his attitude was cooperative with the nurses, so we didn't fight hard enough to stop the nurse from turning him.

"After he died, I stayed with him for a while. The others didn't want to look at him, but I didn't find his appearance disturbing at all. His head was to the side and his jaw was relaxed. I've seen my father almost like that when he was in a deep sleep.

"Throughout my life I had the feeling that I could never do much for my father. He was a self-directed person, very much in control. That was a very central part of his self-esteem. He held himself responsible for anything that happened in his life. This came out of the family he grew up in. He was the tenth of twelve children. Seven are still alive, all crystal clear in their thinking.

"My father was always so directive of everything that when my mother died, he managed everything. We had very little input—except to be children. But it really felt different dealing with his illness and death.

"I read in a chart of life experiences...they give you points for different experiences which, as they added up, meant you were 'more mature.' You got a certain number of points for the loss of a parent, a certain number more for the loss of a second parent. I really appreciate what that means. With both my parents dead, I no longer had anybody else I could fall back on. I'm the only one who has to provide the meaning and direction for others. I feel much more like an adult than I ever have before."

4

Immediately After Death

There is no safe emotional distance from the painful feelings associated with a parent's death. But the closer you've been to your parent during his or her illness, the better you'll feel when death comes. You'll know that you've done your best. Know your own limits; and then accompany your parent as far as you can.

The experiences of family members following a death are a wild mix of feelings and forms; paperwork and grief. Most people struggle to keep from drowning in legal details. One client told me, "After my father's death, I spent two days in my parents' bedroom, dealing with medical and insurance forms."

What do you need to consider in order to prepare for the part that comes after death? Will you be able to take control, or will you be swept away by convention? Convention can be helpful; it creates a structure. But it can also be very costly, and may create meaningless rituals in which you are only an observer and outsider.

In this chapter I will help you handle the time immediately after death; your emotional reactions and feelings, dealing with the undertaker, and arranging the funeral or memorial service and burial.

Reactions and Feelings

Fred had gone to see his 84-year-old father in the hospital every day. He recalls:

> *I was there on my regular visit and it had happened a few hours before. I was stunned. It took my breath away. As much as you expect it, it's a shock. I'm sure I grew very pale. But it had been a slow process and I wasn't overcome with grief.*

Dan remembers:

> *The phone rang. It was my sister. My mother had been rushed to the hospital with a massive cerebral hemorrhage and was brain dead. My mother would have been 80. She had not been ill.*
>
> *I lost it. I cried all night and all the next day. I could barely get dressed to go to the airport. At the airport, I was still crying. I noticed I was surrounded by a lot of tall men and realized it was the Boston Celtics. A 7'3" player sat next to me on the plane. I wanted to put up a macho front, but the feelings just poured out of me. I didn't feel like crying in public, but that was what was happening. I would press my face to the window when the tears came.*

Shea had been traveling back and forth between Michigan and Ohio for over nine months during the course of her father's illness.

My mother called, saying my father had taken a turn for the worse and I needed to come right back. He died while we were driving there. I am convinced to this day I know when he died. I had this incredible sense that my father had died and was stopping by to tell me it was all right—that he'd be dead when I got there and that he was fine.

I'm riding in the car, it's dark and my friend is driving and I've got this feeling. I knew I couldn't tell her. She would think I was absolutely crazy. But it was quite real to me.

When I got to the hospital, the nurse took me to the room where my mother and sister and other relatives were gathered. No one said anything.

I asked if Dad had died, and my mother said yes. I wanted to see him. They took me to his room, and it was not at all like what I expected. It didn't look like my father. He looked very peaceful, though. It was the first time in a long time I'd seen him without pain. I went over, kissed him and stroked his hair. I told him I was very glad that it was over. I was.

Carol had spent the afternoon in the hospital feeding her father lunch. Her brother called her at home in the evening. She needed to come back. Her father was no longer conscious and was having difficulty breathing.

As I was driving down the expressway, I was trying to tell if my father was still alive. It turned out that he died ten minutes before I got there.

When I came into the hospital room, my mother and brother were crying. I touched my father's body. It was very cold. It felt like the spirit was gone out of it. I hadn't been that close before to someone whose spirit was gone. It felt very comfortable.

I remember feeling at that moment I wasn't grieving enough. People would think I wasn't sad enough. I felt that it had all happened very well. I felt gifted to have time with him before he died.

If Your Parent Dies at Home—And You Are Present

The people I interviewed had different experiences following home death. Some were rushed into calling the funeral home long before they were ready to let their parent leave. Others found themselves waiting far too long, with the dead body, for the doctor to sign the death certificate. It seems that things went smoothest when the hospice was involved.

Becky, for instance, credits hospice with making her family's experience less overwhelming:

The hospice people came out and stayed after my father died. They were with us when the men from the mortuary came for the body. It wasn't creepy at all, even though it was the middle of the night. My mother and sister were worried about what it would be like. But it was all so well done. They all really knew what they were doing.

When the mortuary people come to take the body away it is possible to be quite involved. One person I spoke to helped wrap her mother up, then helped lift her and put her in the bag that the mortuary employee was holding. If this process is too upsetting to participate in or even watch, you can simply go into another room.

When my father died in his home, my mother, cousin, and I were the only ones present. We were able to make all the decisions. We waited several hours before we called the doctor and hospice. When we did call, the doctor took care of whatever was necessary by phone, so we did not have to sign a death certificate or deal with bureaucracy.

We had kept my father's hospital bed elevated during the last hours of his life. Not knowing anything about what occurs after death, we simply left him in that semi-upright position. Rigor mortis set in quickly. By the time the two mortuary men arrived from the cremation service, he was stiff and frozen in that position. This made their job more difficult. They had to get a semi-upright body into a bag made for someone lying down.

A few hours after my father died and his body was removed from our home, the medical supply people came to break down the hospital bed and take it away. I remember how empty the room seemed when the hospital bed was gone. First they took my father, then they took his bed. The apartment was back to normal, but we didn't feel the same.

Hospice strongly suggests that you do not call the police, paramedics, or fire department. If you do, they will arrive to check out the death, since all deaths at home are considered suspect. Here is one woman's account of what occurred when her mother died at home and she called the police:

> Immediately following my mother's death, we proceeded as planned. We were to wait 45 minutes, call the police (not 911), report an expected death at home, call the funeral home, and, when the police arrived, we were to give them a signed statement from her doctor that she was in my home to die. The police were supposed to come with no lights, no nothing; and the funeral home would pick her up in an hour. This isn't what happened. The fire department came. The police came—in several police cars— and, of course, Suburban Ambulance. There were lights flashing all the way down the street. At one

point, they implied that we'd have to wait for the medical examiner to pronounce her dead (which could take several hours), after which they'd take her to the county morgue. Needless to say, we were all hysterical.

In the end, they all finally left, but the ambulance insisted on doing an EKG—on a woman who had been dead for over an hour, dragging his junk through my house. It was a nightmare.

If Your Parent Dies in a Hospital or Nursing Home—And You Are Present

Hospitals and nursing homes have set procedures for removing the body and taking care of death certificates. Even so, you can ask to spend time with your parent after he or she has died.

Rosa stayed in the room with her father's body.

I talked to him for a while. I said, "I know you're not here any more. I know you've left us. You're not in your body, but I still want to touch you." Then I kissed his forehead. I felt very lucky to have that time with him. You'd think it would be the one thing you wouldn't want—to actually be there with your parent, dead. But it was a wonderful experience.

Kathryn had a similar experience. She waited outside the room after her mother died for the nurse to clean her mother up and get all the tubes out of the way. "I went back in and was able to have my little conversation with her."

If You Are Not Present When Your Parent Dies

If you are not able to be present when your parent dies, it will be very helpful if you can see your parent's body before it is removed, and say good-bye. If you do not see the body, the death may never seem real to you, and its finality may be more difficult to accept.

Susan was not there when her father died. By the time she flew from Georgia to Florida, her father was no longer at the hospital.

> *They couldn't let me see his body, so I left the hospital. He was dead and I hadn't seen him. I went to the mortuary the next day. But I still couldn't see him. It was like it hadn't really happened. Finally we got there early, the next day, and I could view his body. He looked so wonderful to me. I just cried and cried and cried. I remember exactly how he looked. Peaceful and wise, like he'd grown wiser. It was a comfort to see him, and finally allowed me to express how I was feeling. I wanted to take a picture of him. Now I wish I had.*

Things To Be Done Immediately After Death Occurs

The moment of a parent's death may not be a time when you are thinking very clearly. You may find it useful to make a photocopy of these guidelines for easy reference when you need them.

- When you are ready, notify the mortuary, funeral parlor, or whatever other institution will be responsible for removing the body.

- If you are planning a religious funeral or memorial service, contact the rabbi, priest, or minister.

- Make a list, if you haven't already, of immediate family, close friends, and everyone else you want to notify by phone. If you're not up to it yourself, designate another family member or friend to do the calling.

- Flowers are often sent by well-wishers. If you prefer something different, decide on an appropriate charity or memorial to which gifts can be made in memory of your parent. Funeral notices often specify "Please Omit Flowers."

- Prepare an obituary or death notice to send to your local paper. You can call their obituary department if they have one, and request a blank obituary form. Alternatively, read a few obituaries from the paper to give yourself a sense of the appropriate length and wording. (You may want to ask a friend or family member to do this for you.)

- Obtain a death certificate. This is necessary before cremation or burial can be carried out. You'll need more than one official certified copy (photocopies won't do); you can get these from your local or state health department or county clerk's office. You'll need to present a death certificate for life insurance and pension benefits, to close bank accounts, and to transfer ownership of property. In hospitals, death certificates are provided and signed by the attending doctor. When someone dies at home, the hospice staff will arrange for a death certificate to be prepared.

Things To Be Done in the First Few Days Following Death

- Locate your parent's will. You may want, at this point, to give it to the lawyer who will be handling your parent's estate.

- Notify insurance companies (including auto insurance) of your parent's death. Your initial contact can be by phone, but you'll probably have to write as well.

- Check life insurance, casualty insurance, and death benefits, including Social Security. Death benefits are not always awarded automatically; policies often have time limits for filing. It's important to locate all your parent's policies within the first couple of weeks after death.

Taking care of these details can serve as part of what psychologists call closure. As Shea told me,

> *All the things my mother and I had to do enabled us to come to terms with my father's death. First you call all of his family, then call hers, call the newspaper, call the Veterans Administration, call the insurance company, call the funeral director, organize for the party afterwards. Having those things that have to be done, they kind of anchor you and keep you in motion.*

Making Funeral and Burial Arrangements

This is a period when you especially want to do the right thing. And yet if you haven't had a lot of experience planning previous funerals (and I hope you haven't), "the right thing" usually means doing what everybody else does.

Considering some of the options beforehand—preferably in consultation with your parent—will be of great help in carrying out what's appropriate in your particular situation when the time comes.

Some people are glad to have others do this job; and some prefer to make all the funeral arrangements themselves. You have to ask yourself how involved you want to be. How much involvement can you handle?

In the sections that follow, I will sketch out the options of burial and cremation, explore the issues that can arise when making funeral decisions in consultation with other family members, and discuss the planning of funerals and memorial services. First, though, it may be useful for you to consider the following questions.

- What would your parent have wanted in the way of funeral arrangements? What wishes did your parent express before he/she died?

- What will have the most emotional meaning for you?

- What best meets the needs of other family members? (Is this in conflict with what you want?)

- What are the costs of the various alternatives? (Is cost an issue?)

Bear in mind that spending a lot of money is not necessarily a way of showing respect. Real ostentation at funerals tells more about the status consciousness of the surviving family members than it does about their attachment to the deceased. Of course, funeral traditions vary greatly from culture to culture: what is "right" for your family might not be right for another. As with weddings and other rites of passage in this country, there is a vast range of possibilities.

Knowing Your Options

As far as we know, the tradition of human burial began 60,000 years ago, when the Neanderthals started placing their dead in the earth, then covering them with rocks and dirt.

Cremation was introduced by the Greeks about 1000 B.C. Enemies were desecrating the bodies of their dead soldiers. To protect them, the Greeks cremated the bodies and shipped the ashes home.

Nowadays you have a choice, although in the United States burial continues to be the more common practice. If you decide to bury your parent and have a funeral, using a conventional funeral parlor and funeral director, this is what your costs may be (costs range greatly, depending on the "going rates" for your geographic region, and the quantity or supposed quality of the product or service involved):

- Embalming (a common practice, but not necessary or legally required): $95-$380

- Refrigeration (an alternative to embalming): $45-$125

- Cosmetic preparation of the body: $65-$235

- Burial clothing: $35-$100

- Visitation room rental fee: $45-$260

- Chapel rental: $95-$200

- Honoraria for clergy: $25-$250

- Hearse: $95-$125

- Casket: $200 (plain pine or particleboard) to $15,000 (for a metal casket)

- Total: $700-$16,675*

As these figures show, the casket is often the most expensive part of the funeral. Jessica Mitford's 1963 book, *The American Way of Death*, did much to reform the funeral industry in this country, which was rife with corrupt sales practices. Read it if you have a strong stomach and are in the mood for a bellyful of black humor.

Dealing with funeral directors and funeral parlors can be difficult, because people who are basically salesmen are casting

*Figures taken from *Affairs in Order*, by Patricia Anderson.

themselves in the role of grief counselors. Shea remembers her trip to the undertaker:

> *The man was very nice. He brought us into this little room and put out coffee, Italian pastries, and shot glasses, and talked to us for a while. But then he took us into this room that contained all the caskets. There you are trying to figure out some way to talk about it to one another. And there's no vocabulary for what makes a casket good; so you use the language you use for talking about cars— "Nice upholstery, great color." My mother, my sister, and my aunt Jofie and I made this excursion, and God knows how we ever decided on which casket to buy.*

The funeral home usually "fixes up" and embalms the body. "Whatever they do to people," said one woman, "it's terrible. My father looked really different. They had some kind of paste or wax on his eyes to keep them shut. I was really glad I had spent several hours with him after he died, because he just didn't look like himself in the casket. It's subtle things—like they parted his hair on the wrong side."

Burying Your Own

Taking care of the dead used to be a family or community activity. Now almost everybody turns to funeral directors and funeral parlors to handle the details, because they feel too upset and confused to handle arrangements themselves.

And yet there are other options. Some religious and ethnic groups, like the Amish and the Mennonites, still handle their own funeral and disposition arrangements without professional assistance. In traditional Judaism, *Hevra Kadish*, a special committee of experienced volunteers, prepare the body for burial. Other communities of people in this country have formulated similar arrangements for caring for their dead. It's actually possible to handle everything yourself—from obtaining the death certificate and getting proper permits, to transportation and burial. If you think that you might want to handle these arrangements yourself, read Lisa Carlson's book, *Caring for Your Own Dead.*

My friend Maria's father died in a hospital. The family wanted to take him home, have a wake, and then bury him. It was their family's tradition to bury people from their own homes.

The funeral parlor they contacted had never been asked to do so little—really to stay out of the picture—but they were willing to cooperate.

Because Maria's family would have been uncomfortable viewing her father's naked body, they had the funeral people take him from the hospital to the funeral parlor to dress him. (Of course, they could have opted to wash and dress him themselves.)

They called a carpenter in town and asked him to make a simple wooden box, with no upholstery. Maria, her mother, and her eight brothers and sisters put a clean pillowcase on the pillow from her father's bed, then spent the afternoon cutting up foam rubber for the coffin. There was a lot of going back and forth trying to find something appropriate to bury him in.

My mother went upstairs and came down with a three-piece suit—my brother's wedding suit. We laughed. My brother's wife would be pretty upset if Pop was laid out in Mark's wedding suit. So we decided on an old brown jacket, white shirt, and tie—clothes my father would have worn when he had to get dressed up.

We prepared the casket right in the middle of our living room. The kids climbed in and out of it; we got in and tried it out. Jokes were made.

When the casket was ready, we put it on the back of the truck and brought it to the funeral home. We had wanted him minimally embalmed, with no makeup. I remember they did something to his lungs, so he wouldn't have spittle coming out of his mouth. But he looked totally like himself. They put Pop in the casket and brought him back to our house. Meanwhile, we had gotten the living room ready: taken out family picture albums, things that were special to Pop—pictures, his favorite crucifix, articles from his barn, shop, garage, and hung them up against the wall where the casket was.

We opened the casket and put his rosary and prayer book in. Then we went out and gathered flowers from our garden and the road. This was Sunday. That afternoon we had an open house. Everyone came and was able to say good-bye. When they all left, we discussed whether we should close the casket or leave it open during the night. We decided to close it. That night we all slept in the house, with Pop's body there, too.

The next morning, we had the grandkids draw pictures, write notes, and make anything they wanted to tuck into the casket. Then we opened the casket and they put in all their little things.

The funeral people came and screwed the top back on. We asked them to be a very minor presence, so they only appeared and helped when asked.

Then, with our help, the funeral people carried the casket to the car. They had not brought a hearse; and we were glad about that. But they had a ramshackle station wagon, usually used to pick up bodies from the hospital. We had to laugh.

They took the body to the church, where we had a traditional funeral mass.

We had arranged for someone to dig the hole at the cemetery, and had requested no carpeting or cover-up, and to please leave some dirt. At the gravesite, the priest said a traditional Catholic prayer. The funeral home people lowered the casket into the ground. We all carried flowers that we tossed down onto the casket. Then, with shovels we had brought from home, everyone who wanted to was able to shovel some dirt over the casket, while others sang songs. We felt like we were, at least symbolically, burying our own dead, even though we did not fill the entire hole.

Afterwards, there was no feeling that the living room was "weird or spooky" because it had been used for the wake. What seems weird is to leave the body of someone you care about all alone in a chilly, sterile, unfamiliar funeral home.

Cremation

Why consider cremation? Cemetery land is becoming very expensive and very scarce. This fact, as well as the enormous expense of caskets and funeral preparations, makes it a lot less expensive to cremate someone. Ashes can then be placed in a container or funeral urn for burial or storage, or scattered in a place that has some meaning or special association for your parent.

My father had let us know that he wanted to be cremated. Being the kind of family that always shopped for bargains and was very frugal, this seemed a fitting way for him to go. My father's cremation cost $266—quite a bit less than the usual $3,000-$5,000 funeral!

We got the name of our crematorium from hospice. I remember the car ride down to sign papers. We tried to imagine what we were going to see. It turned out to be a small office in a shopping mall, obviously the place where paperwork took place, not anything else. The man who was in charge had a very matter-of-fact attitude.

Each state has its own rules governing where and how you can scatter funeral ashes. These rules, however, are often difficult to enforce. I came across this story in a newspaper: "The family would hate to say they sprinkled their father's ashes on the 18th green of his favorite golf course, because they think that might be illegal. But they will say, that's what their father would have wanted."

Scattering the ashes of your parent's body will be a moving experience, whether you choose the seaside, a mountain, or your own backyard. Because you are taking the ritual literally into your own hands, you will get a full sense of closure, ashes to ashes, dust to dust.

Local funeral directors, hospice, and the yellow pages of your phone book are good sources of information about crematoriums in your area.

It's Not Always Easy for Families to Agree

Sometimes family members are in complete accord about funeral and memorial arrangements for a parent who has died. But emotions run high at such times, and old resentments have a way of surfacing. It's not at all uncommon for bitter antagonism among family members to dog the decision-making process at every step of the way.

One woman's father had asked to be cremated and have the ashes scattered, but her brother wanted there to be a gravesite that he could visit with his children. After the cremation, they had many heated discussions over what she came to think of as the scatter-versus-bury controversy. They were unable to agree. "The upshot is that my father's ashes are still in a box in his bedroom. In a Japanese box in an urn, neither buried nor scattered, but not exactly kept in a way that honors him. There's the exercise bicycle, magazines, and the urn in the box."

Another woman recalls how her grandfather explicitly requested that his ashes be scattered over the hillside of the home where he'd lived for many years, and where his daughter was living now. But the daughter was so completely traumatized by the idea of the ashes themselves that she couldn't even bear to go to the crematorium to get them. The idea of having her father's mortal remains scattered outside her bedroom window sent her into complete hysterics. Meanwhile, the grandfather's sister, a formidable lady in her nineties, was so offended that her brother had been cremated at all (it was against her religion) that she refused to speak to her niece, whom she held responsible for the arrangements. The ashes were finally buried, not scattered, on another relative's property, in a ceremony that didn't include the granddaughter or her great aunt.

Rosa quickly realized that she could either suffer through a series of terrible arguments with her mother, who had become a victim of "doing the right thing," or she could keep her mouth shut. Her father had wanted to be cremated, but never formalized that decision. So he ended up being buried. And instead of a simple pine box, which she knew her father would have preferred, her mother thought "it wouldn't look right"—so they spent money on a fairly expensive casket.

> I also had to wear black and I didn't want to; I wanted to wear white. I had brought along this high-fashion white suit, which I knew my father would have loved. I wanted to wear it to his funeral, but my mother wouldn't let me: "What would the neighbors say?" It was an uninspired funeral service, and it was painful to me because I thought he deserved better. But I had to butt out of it or else my mother and I would have been constantly fighting.
>
> Even the cemetery was horrible. There were no upright stones. They were all flat, so that it would be easier to mow the lawn. I felt outraged. I had wanted my father to have a very simple but beautiful stone, and here was this ugly cemetery plot you could hardly tell was a cemetery; even now and again you'd discover you'd been walking on someone's grave. I spent a lot of time trying to find

someplace beautiful in this totally unappealing
place. He was going to be there forever, or at least
some of his remains were. My mother got very im-
patient, but I finally did manage to find a slightly
more pleasant spot.

I stayed down in Florida for a couple of more
days after the funeral, and spent a lot of time alone,
just looking up at the sky, feeling that he was up
there, and talking to him in Yiddish. My Yiddish
had come back to me so I could talk to him and it
felt really nice.

In choosing what to argue about and what to let go, keep in mind that the funeral and burial ceremonies are over quickly, but your relationship with the rest of your family will last a lifetime.

Funerals and Memorial Services

Ernest Morgan, in *Dealing Creatively with Death*, lists a number of social and emotional needs that death rituals can meet for survivors:

- Reestablishing relationships with others in the community so that life can resume for the living in a more normal way

- Identifying and echoing the values of the deceased

- Affirming your own values in the face of another's death

- Relief from guilt

- Rehabilitation of the memory of the deceased, especially after a long and disfiguring illness

- Opportunity to deepen religious and spiritual life

- Sharing in one another's emotional support, encouragement, and strength

"Before my mother's death," said Toby, "I never understood how important a memorial service is. It doesn't just provide for you and your family—it provides for everybody. It was so helpful to us to see who cared about my mother, and to cry and remember. It cemented the people of this community into my heart."

Some people consider funeral and memorial customs to be morbid; others consider them helpful. It's common to have ambivalent feelings about any such rituals.

Catherine couldn't understand why the family of the person who died has to give a party and serve people food and drinks. It seemed gruesome to her. "Your mother dies and you have a death party." But she didn't feel she could take a stand and refuse to have a wake for her mother. Later, she says, she was glad that she'd held the wake after all, because she liked the way it felt, being at her house with people who really cared about her mother.

If possible, the funeral or memorial service should be held in a familiar place—your home, your parents' home, your church or temple—instead of at a funeral parlor.

This is not always possible. Kathryn found herself having to make funeral arrangements in a strange town. She relied a lot on the local mortician. Finally, the nursing home her mother had been in volunteered to have a little "coffee celebration" as a memorial service. They organized the whole thing.

If you do use a funeral home, you can do little things to make the atmosphere more personal, so everyone feels less alienated. One man discovered that seeing his father dead wasn't as disturbing as seeing him laid out in the coffin.

I didn't like the way they had him made up. It wasn't natural. My nephew kept saying that it didn't look like grandpa; only the hands looked like grandpa. And that was what I was thinking. The

hands and the hair and ears were his, but the face
as it had been made up didn't look like him at all.
So what I did was bring in a big smiling picture of
my father. It was about 14 x 20 and I put it where
everyone could look at it.

One family brought origami cranes (symbols of longevity and healing) that had been hung in their father's hospital room, and draped them over the casket. "Just before we closed the casket, we tucked them inside, along with notes from the children that we stuck under his pillow."

One woman I interviewed served as a pallbearer for her father's coffin, along with her brothers. "It was very hard for me," she recalls. "I was sobbing the whole time, and it was heavy carrying the casket through the narrow corridors and down the stairs. I was in shambles, but I felt really glad to be able to do it."

Another woman stuck notes into her father's pockets as he lay in an open casket. "I didn't want to appear crazy," she told me, "so I did it secretly." She was to find out later that her 15-year-old daughter had done exactly the same thing. They had both felt the pull to give him something personal to take with him—wherever he was going.

One client, whose father had molested her when she was young, wrote a long letter describing how she had learned to forgive him. She slipped the letter into his open casket, and felt comforted believing he would know what it said.

A memorial service can be used as a forum for telling stories about your parent, giving some sense of what he or she was like. This is a good way to have people participate in, rather than just watch, the funeral. But getting up and saying something in public can be very difficult. Many feel too close to tears to speak. They are often relieved that someone else—the minister, rabbi, or priest—is handling the service.

Unless the person officiating is someone you know well, it's not always possible to know what kind of job they'll do.

There's nothing worse at a moment of great emotion than to have some stranger spouting clichés about your parent, or missing the point completely. When the minister handling her mother's service made uninspired and impersonal comments, one woman I spoke to coped by focusing on the little urn that contained her mother's ashes. "I blocked everything else out."

Another woman I interviewed had been very upset with the rabbi who, despite close involvement with the family, gave a pretty standard eulogy, "like eulogy number 33." So afterwards, she got up and read her own eulogy that she'd written many months before, when she first learned that her father was ill. "People were really touched. I don't know if they were touched so much by what I said, or by the fact I actually got up there and said it."

If the person officiating *didn't* know your parent, take the time to communicate what *you'd* like to have stressed in the service. Most people will be responsive to your efforts (and, if they're not, you should find someone else). Give as many personal details as you can about your parent; tell touching or funny stories that reveal your parent as an individual. This can be a good opportunity to get together with other members of your family to gather notes for the priest, minister, or rabbi.

Like so many others, my family was not a real part of the community they retired in and had no regular religious institution they belonged to. So, once again, we relied on hospice help. They told me about an unaffiliated rabbi, someone who did not belong to a particular congregation. I called to ask if he would perform the service. He spent over 45 minutes with me on the phone, asking questions about my father. In a way, this conversation with the rabbi felt to me like *my* eulogy. In sharing with someone the details of my father's life, and his contribution to mine, I was able to give a speech about my father without having to do so at the service. The rabbi was able to give larger voice to my feelings when he spoke, sharing the information I'd given him.

We decided to hold the memorial service in my parents' condominium. My father had been president, and was known and liked by many people there. Also, many of his friends were old, without vehicles or no longer driving. Our choice of location meant they wouldn't have to travel to attend.

The condominium association gave us a large meeting room overlooking the pool. My cousin and aunt took care of providing coffee and cake, so my mother and I had little to do. We put a notice up on the bulletin board and called several close friends.

It went well. Lots of people came. The rabbi was wonderful and because of our long conversation, sounded as if he knew my father. He also allowed time for others to talk and share their memories.

But for me, it was a morning to get through. I felt like a hostess, worried about all the details. Would the rabbi arrive on time? Would things go well? I was very nervous and knew that I was not going to be able to mourn there. I did not feel comfortable crying in that setting. But it was a place that had real meaning for my father and mother, and it was a good choice for everyone else involved.

References

Anderson, Patricia (1991) *Affairs in Order: A Complete Guide to Death and Dying*. New York: MacMillan Publishing Company.

Carlson, Lisa (1987) *Caring for Your Own Dead*. Hinesburg, VT: Upper Access Publishers.

Mitford, Jessica (1963) *The American Way of Death*. New York: Fawcett Crest.

Morgan, Ernest (1988) *Dealing Creatively with Death: A Manual of Death Education and Simple Burial* (11th revised edition). Burnsville, NC: Celo Press.

Shea's Story

Shea is single and lives in Detroit, where she is a professor of speech and communication at Oakland University. She grew up in a small town in Ohio, where her younger sister and mother still live.

Shea's father, John, was a miner and foundry worker. After he developed a tremor in his hand, he found work in Ohio organizing credit unions.

He was 65 when he became ill with throat cancer. He died nine months later in the hospital.

"My father was very warm, gregarious, talkative—a storyteller. And he loved to sing. He was easy to get along with and very oriented to our family. Like many men, he had few really close friends; but for 40 years he kept in contact with someone he had been close to during the war. Another friend, from his high school days, reappeared during his illness and was a tremendous source of support.

"My father and I were very close and had a good relationship. We shared a lot. He taught me how to play ball and fix things. We spent a lot of time together when I was growing up. He told me lots of stories about when he was a kid. It was easy for us, because I liked to do the things he liked to do.

"We had an open relationship. My father dealt with things as they were. He didn't really spend a lot of time on how he felt about them. Once, many years before, he said he was not afraid of dying, because in World War II he faced death a lot. He would have liked to travel, retire, and do all that, but I don't think he felt there were things left untended. He didn't lead his life that way.

"In December of 1983, when I got my Ph.D., my mother and father came to my graduation. When we were driving in the car, I wanted my father to sing, because one of my fondest childhood memories was that my father was a wonderful singer; he often sang. But he couldn't that day, because he had a sore throat. I somehow felt like it was something more—if it was just a sore throat, he would sing anyway. He retired two months later, because he still wasn't feeling well. Shortly after, he was diagnosed with throat cancer: he had a tumor attached to the artery going to the brain. He died not quite a year later.

"My friends Susan and Jane were incredibly helpful. Susan's father had died three years before. I had seen a lot of what she did and her family did. They were all very direct with one another in a good way. You need to be able to speak about what is happening and what you feel—I might not have known otherwise.

"Seeing the way Susan's father withdrew from the world—from news, books, and current events—his desire to connect with people seemed to dwindle. There's only so much energy a dying person has. If I hadn't seen that already, it would have been a shock to me seeing it in my father.

"Jane's father had died six months before. There were a lot of similarities in our situation and problems—like, how do you cope when you have to travel? My parents lived five hours away. It's not like after work you can stop at the hospital or go by the house.

"I was able to understand some of my reactions. This didn't stop them, but it was comforting to understand them, and to understand my mother, particularly her anger. My parents had never exchanged angry words. To see the anger in my mother at my father's illness…it could have been a real stickler. Jane told me what to look out for—and these things gave me real direction, so I was better able to handle my mother's reactions, as well as my own.

"Then we started this long process. Through my whole growing up, we never went to doctors. Nobody in my family did. So all of us were very unprepared for dealing with doctors. After they operated and found out for sure it was cancer, they said they needed to open his windpipe, because of the fear that he would suffocate. So they cut a hole in his throat and put in a tube for him to breathe through. And what happened is, he never got his voice back. If there was ever a time he needed to talk and interact, it was then; but this damn tube really cut his ability to communicate. So much of his sense of self had been his ability to tell stories and engage in conversation. But this tube made it very difficult for him to speak. I really think, once he lost his voice, a whole part of himself died, much before he died. He became so silent, it was hard to talk about things. If I hadn't had a good, open relationship with him, that would have been so much harder to deal with.

"In that whole period, we only had one really intense interaction. We were watching the news together, and I made some crack, and he made some comment. Then he followed it up by saying it didn't really matter what he thought because his life hadn't amounted to much anyway. And I got furious at him. I yelled about how he shouldn't say that about himself. So he stopped. We had one of those moments of connection. Then somebody came in. Most of what I remember about that whole time is his slow disappearance: physically my father started to get much smaller and more frail.

"Then there was a series of trips in and out of the hospital, and I was traveling hack home every other weekend, five hours each way. In the hospital it's amazing how small your world becomes. The things that matter are what you eat, what time the nurse comes, whether or not the doctor's been there. And the doctor would say he was going to come and then he wouldn't. And we would feel so powerless. On the one hand, you look to this guy to save your father, and on the other hand he was such a jerk and very unresponsive.

"There was one terrible scene. The doctor came in with a group of medical students and called my father by his first name with a very condescending attitude. He told my father to stand up and proceeded to discuss the surgery on the side of his neck. Then he walked out, leaving my father standing there. It was as though he wasn't even a person—just a neck. That's the kind of thing in a hospital that really contributes to wearing a person down. About the only people who seemed to care were the nurses. The doctors…you wanted to see them, but when you did you were sorry you had. They were awful.

"They operated on my father, but it was a failure. They couldn't remove the tumor, because it had started to go into this blood vessel that went up to the brain. So that was that. That was the end of what the doctors could do. The only good thing was that we were able to take my father home for a while.

"At home he had a hard time. Physically, he was in a lot of pain and he couldn't do even simple things. Basic movement was hard for him, so walking from one room to another became almost impossible.

"And he became really isolated, because he couldn't use his voice to talk or sing. Ordinary ways of interacting were confined because of this mechanical thing in his throat. I found myself worrying a lot about my mother. They were the center of one another's lives: how was she going to handle the loss?

"Once he lost his voice, there was a real sense of resignation in him, which wasn't what he'd been like during the rest of his life. Because he was in tremendous pain, the doctor talked about amputating his leg. My father said absolutely not. And we all agreed. He didn't want to die in pieces. He couldn't handle it. But he ended up back in the hospital because they were going to have to operate to relieve a blood clot. But before they could, he died. I got a phone call from my mother to come as quickly as possible. But he was dead when I got there.

"Afterwards, we all went back to my parents' house. They had a small house and it was packed with relatives. There was lots of laughter, lots of stories, and lots of crying.

"I think the hardest part was not so much his dying, but after he was dead. The people who are there, like my mother and sister…they're there all the time, so they can sort of adjust. But I was thrown into emotional turmoil. We had had a long-distance relationship. Much of my going home was to see him. For a year or more, every time I went home to visit, I'd be expecting to see him and he wouldn't be there."

5

Adjusting to the Loss

The burial, funeral, or memorial service is a turning point. You move from close interaction with your parent to a place where interaction is no longer possible. You are left with your own feelings, doubts, regrets, and memories, and perhaps with questions that will forever remain unanswered.

To say good-bye, to come to peace with individual death, is really the way in which you come to learn more about your spiritual self.

Within each person there is some power, some spirit, some living energy that is more than the accumulation of the working parts of your body.

This chapter will help you call forth that something more—that power that comes from within you—and allow you to use it.

Most people in our society don't know how to gather together their spiritual assets to use during difficult times. People can see, and often use, their material wealth. With money, you can buy an expensive coffin for your parent, a vacation or a massage for yourself—things that may help. But you need more.

There's a wonderful passage in *The Education of Little Tree*, Forrest Carter's remembrances of his Eastern Cherokee hill country grandparents, that talks about what that "more" is:

> *Granma said everybody has two minds. One of the minds has to do with the necessaries for body living. You had to use it to figure how to get shelter and eating and such like for the body. She said you had to use it to mate and have young 'uns and such. She said, we had to have that mind so as we could carry on. But she said we had another mind that had nothing at all to do with such. She said it was a spiritual mind.*
>
> *Granma said that the spirit mind was like any other muscle. If you used it it got bigger and stronger. She said the only way it could get that way was using it to understand...then understanding commenced to take up, and the more you tried to understand, the bigger it got.*

Exercising the spirit mind is a lot like exercising the body. It requires commitment. It requires discipline.

Trying To Understand

You must come to know what you think about death. I watched my father die, and sat with him for several hours after his death. For a while, it seemed that he was still there, in the room. Then it felt as if he was gone. His body was still on the bed, but my father was not in it. For the first time, I began to think about what happens after the body dies. Did my father's spirit die, too? If not, where did it go? Was death the end, or simply a transition?

This is a time to think and talk about death. Open yourself up to all your questions and fears. This may make you feel upset; but, as one friend said to me, "It's a good upset. It feels like growth."

One woman I interviewed, whose parent died unexpectedly, decided to attend a workshop on death and dying that made use of videotapes featuring Ram Dass and Stephen Levine. "Conscious Living/Conscious Dying" helped her explore her personal reactions to her parent's death. She describes herself

> *weighted down with amulets, wood to knock on*
> *every time the word death came up, my fingers*
> *permanently crossed, carrying my lucky number. I*
> *went off to spend a weekend in the presence of the*
> *word death. I brought my amulets to protect me*
> *from the impact of that word. I left no longer*
> *needing them.*

This is also a good time to read *Who Dies*, by Stephen Levine. It's an enormously comforting book.

Finding Comfort

In our microwave culture, we expect everything to get done quickly. But it's best to move slowly now. Don't rush to "adjust."

This is a time of sadness. Acknowledge it. Don't pretend to be all right. Don't put on a good face. Don't go right back to work if you don't have to. You may feel disoriented. One friend told me, "I went back to my job the day after the funeral. I looked at my telephone messages and started to cry." If possible, make a space in your life—a time you can feel grief, a time you're not expected to be any way at all. If you do have to go back to a job or family responsibilities right away, then develop some rituals for remembering your parent and honoring your feelings.

Spend time with nature. Every day for the first month, watch the sunrise and the sunset. For the whole year, closely observe the cycle of seasons. Notice how winter always follows spring.

As our culture has moved further and further away from nature—the most visible source of the divine, the soul of the universe—we have lost touch with our best teacher. The seasons of nature are our most constant reminder that life has cycles. We ignore what we see in our own backyards: birth, blossoming, fading, and dying. Over and over and over again.

Allow yourself time to hurt. This is a dark time. Don't try to escape your painful feelings. But create an environment that supports you. Take special care of yourself. You need to rest a lot. But you also need to keep busy, to wear yourself out, so that you can let go of some of the pain.

Physically, you may feel a tightness in your throat, a heaviness in your chest, loss of appetite, an emptiness inside, or terrible restlessness.

There is no right way to feel. I cried more before my father died than afterwards. I did not feel grief-stricken. I took a week off. I stared into space. Read mysteries. Cleaned the basement. I felt more off-balance than anything else. Then several years later, in the spring when my daughter won her first track meet, I found myself sobbing uncontrollably. I wanted to call my father to tell him this exciting news. But I could no longer reach him by telephone.

Tips To Help You Get Through this Dark Time: A Guide for the First Few Months

During dark times it is not unusual to feel like you are off-balance, falling apart, breaking down. This is a time to rest. A time to question. A time to learn.

1. Create a space and time to allow yourself to read books, listen to tapes, or watch videos on death and dying. (See resource chapter for suggestions.)

2. Develop your own rituals for remembering. Light a candle. Say a prayer. Take a walk alone. Sit outside and look at the stars.

3. Share stories. Seek out friends or relatives whose parents have died. Talk about your experience. Listen to theirs.

4. Sleep a lot if you need to. Withdrawing, sleeping, needing time alone are common reactions during the few months after a loss. One client of mine was frightened by her reactions. She was working, coming home, and going to bed—sleeping more than she ever had in the past. She didn't return calls from friends or relatives. She avoided everyone. She told me, "I don't even want to be with my closest friends."

5. Let your feelings out. I've often told clients, if you bury your feelings inside, they will eventually come out, either disguised as strange feelings or strange behavior. Or else the weight and energy of those unexpressed feelings will begin to cause you physical problems. The energy has to go somewhere. It's better to release it directly.

6. Focus on your own health. How well do you take care of yourself? Do you know your cholesterol level? Your hemoglobin (iron count)? Your blood pressure? These can all give you some important information about your own body, and physical health.

Each month, choose a different health goal. If you eat too many sweets and too much sugar, then spend one month working on reducing your sugar intake. If you are always stressed out and physically on edge, concentrate on deep relaxation and learning how to meditate.

Remember—everyone is different. There are five billion people and not one of us has the exact same fingerprint. Why assume that we have the exact same ways of responding to loss? Whatever your feelings are, they are the right and appropriate feelings for you at this moment in time.

Dreaming

Dreaming, and remembering your dreams, can play a big part in exercising your spirit mind. It can help you understand what you are thinking and feeling.

For a long time after her father's death, one woman I interviewed had frequent nightmares about being murdered. Even though she had completely accepted what happened, on a deeper level she remained shocked by death, even by death in old age. "It felt to me very much like a murder had taken place."

A friend of mine dreamt about her mother every night for the first few months after she died. One night she would relive the horror of her mother's death; the next night she would dream that her mother hadn't died—she was fine and nothing was wrong. The worst dream she had was one in which her mother came back but then she said she had to go. In that dream, my friend woke up sobbing, "Please don't go. Please stay."

Dan's father died in 1961. Since that time, at least once a year, he's been having what he's come to think of as his "denial of death" dream:

> *My family is all together. My mother and sister and I, doing something, but my father's not with us. He's left us and is living with another woman, somewhere else. But I'm always expecting him to return, and feel perplexed and angry that he's not present.*

Every dream Shea had for months after her father's death took place in a hospital. During the day, she sometimes found that she would be looking at people and all she could see were skeletons. She was scared. She thought she was going crazy. But her imagination was so imprinted by the illness and death of her father that she couldn't get loose. Then she had this dream:

> *It was sort of like this movie,* State Fair. *It was a musical comedy starring my father and mother, who sang and danced. And in the end, it was very much like Dale Evans and Roy Rogers, sort of* Happy Trails *and waving good-bye, and the credits rolling by, with my father singing and waving. And since that time I've had no more bad dreams.*

I kept waiting to have my musical comedy dream. But instead it was my friend Phil who had a healing dream for me. He called me early one morning to tell it to me.

He dreamed we were all at my home. The phone rings. Phil answers it. It's my father and he asks to speak with me. As Phil hands me the phone, he sees that I already know who is calling. I take the call upstairs. Phil and my husband listen in. They want to be sure that my father, who has died, is actually calling on the phone. My father talks with me. He begins to talk about tartar sauce. After a few minutes we are disconnected. I come back downstairs. Phil realizes that the whole point of the call is that my father wants to let me know how proud he is of me, and of how I cared for him. He didn't have a chance to thank me.

Phil is crying as he tells me this last part. He can barely talk. He doesn't really know how I cared for my father, as I was in San Diego and Phil was here in Michigan. He also does not know that my father was an extremely picky eater, and *never* ate tartar sauce until the last few months of his life (then to his surprise, he liked it). I don't know what to think. But I do know what I feel: connected to my father who is dead.

That connection does not end when parents die. It simply changes as you find ways to adjust to their absence from your daily life.

Dreamwork

- Pay attention to your dreams.

- Keep a pad and pencil by your bed. Write your dreams down as soon as you wake up.

- Spend some time contemplating what your dreams might mean.

Opening Up to Your Own Mortality

Accepting another person's death is hard; learning to accept your own mortality is even harder. One friend of mine watched her mother die; and then, a year and a half later, her 50-year-old brother died of lung cancer. "I never believed that anyone I knew would die," she told me. "Now I'm learning to accept that people get ill and die, even my own mother and brother. But me, I mean, *I'm* not going to die!"

Many people feel the same way. Yet many of those I interviewed found that the experience of dealing with their parent's death opened them up to a newly awakened consciousness of their own mortality. This didn't make them more afraid; but did give them a stronger sense of appreciation for their own lives.

When Kathryn's mother died at age 84 after a long illness, Kathryn found herself having this treadmill image over and over again:

> *On the treadmill in front of you is your grand-*
> *mother, then your grandfather, then your mother*
> *and father. The treadmill keeps moving. First your*
> *grandpa falls off, then your grandma, then your*

daddy and mommy and all of a sudden you're in
the front of the line and you're going to go off next.
It's not so much fear of death. It's more like you
start to ask, "Where am I? Am I where I want to
be?"

Trying to deal with your parent's death can leave you more able to think about your own death, and therefore your own life.

A Spiritual Growth Spurt

Although I have thought a lot about death since my own father died, I still don't feel as if I understand the meaning of death. But what his death has made me think about even more profoundly is the meaning of life.

A hospice nurse once told me that she learned a lot by being with so many people who die. She has never heard anyone facing death say, "I wish I had had more Mercedes." Instead, they say such things as, "I wish I had had a better relationship with my family." "I wish I had enjoyed life more."

One client of mine who was diagnosed with a fatal illness asked me, "What is the meaning of life? What is the meaning of my life?" This is a question all of us need to ask ourselves. Not when we are about to die, but when we still have time to be the heroes rather than the victims of our lives.

Exercises for Opening Up to Yourself: Learning What's Important to You

1. Imagine that you are 90 years old, and you are looking back at your life. Think about what you hope to have accomplished. What would make you feel proud? What contributed to your happiness?

2. Start setting life goals for yourself. Chart a course: make positive statements about what you are going to work on. What do you hope to accomplish in:

Three months? _____

_____

Six months?_____

_____

One year? _____

_____

Five years?_____

_____

Ten years? _____

_____

3. Examine your work life, home life, and relationships. Ask yourself these questions (use extra paper if you need it):

Do I feel stuck in relationships or situations I don't like?_____

_____

Do I feel like I am drifting—not in control of my own life and what's happening to me?_____

_____

What makes me happy? _____

_____

What makes me feel satisfied?_____

What makes me feel productive? _____

What would make me feel successful?_____

What are my present priorities? Does my schedule reflect these priorities? _____

And Finally...

I continue some six years later to recognize my father's death day. My husband and children accompany me to temple on the Friday closest to October 24th, so I can rise and repeat the Jewish prayer for the dead, the Kaddish. I take comfort in this ritual and reminder of how much I miss my father in my everyday life. I have adjusted, but I have not gotten over it.

I listen, again, to the rabbi's words, "May he rest in peace"; and recall how I noticed, a short time after my father's death, at the dinner table one evening, when someone said something funny, that I laughed with a new laugh—my father's laugh. It was then I realized that my father is resting—inside of me. At least that's where his laugh is.

References

Carter, Forrest (1976) *The Education of Little Tree.* New York: Delacorte Press.

Ram Dass and Stephen Levine. "How Shall We Live?" A video series on personal awakening and planetary survival produced by Original Face Video, 6116 Merced Avenue, #165, Oakland, CA 94611; phone (510) 339-3126.

Levine, Stephen (1982) *Who Dies? An Investigation of Conscious Living and Conscious Dying.* Garden City, NY: Anchor Press/Doubleday.

Toby's Story

Toby has his own sewing machine repair business, and teaches high school environmental science part-time in a small town in Michigan. He's divorced, and has joint custody of his three young children.

Toby's mother Barbara was an artist, writer, and radical. She created murals and worked with the WPA, was a supporter of the Flint sit-down strike, lived collectively in the 30s, and was part of the antiwar movement in the 60s. She was also a recovering alcoholic. Her husband, John, also a lifelong radical, had been an auto mechanic.

Toby and his younger sister, Lisa, took major responsibility for their mother's care. Lisa was living with Barbara when she became ill. Their older brother, Jim, who lived in Illinois, visited as often as he could.

During the last stage of their mother's life, each child was able to find a special way of relating to her. Toby took macrobiotic cooking lessons with her—he had always enjoyed food and cooking. Jim, who had studied and taught Transcendental Meditation, helped her learn to meditate. Lisa, a trained myomassologist, gave her mother massages.

Toby had already had direct experience with death: his grandmother died at home when he was 38; two years later, Toby's 82-year-old father had a heart attack and died while splitting wood.

Although Toby's mother had cancer for 12 years, most of that time it was in remission. Then her dentist found a new tumor, and she was diagnosed with mouth cancer. She became bedridden and died about two months later, at the age of 76.

"Around Christmastime, my mother became very ill and couldn't leave her bed. That's when we contacted hospice. They helped us take care of her for the next ten weeks.

"We could see that her vitality was slipping. She let us know that she'd resigned herself to dying. Accepted it. She told my brother that she realized she was beginning to let go of worldly values. The week before, when she was having problems keeping her dentures in, she still felt very self-conscious about taking them out in front of people. Now she took her dentures out while she was talking and said, 'You know, this doesn't bother me. I'm beginning to let go.' This led to a discussion about death.

"A few days later, my sister Lisa called me at work, early in the morning. She said the hospice nurse didn't think my mother had long to live. So I dropped what I was doing, lined up a babysitter, and went right over to my mother's house.

"I went into her room. It was about 11:15 a.m. I could tell she was in a different state. Her eyes were closed, but she was still conscious, and I sensed that she could tell I was there. It was a beautiful day, the sun was shining, and she looked very peaceful. She wasn't really in pain, but her breath was getting irregular. I was the only one in the room. I sat by her side, watching her and saying a prayer. Then I realized I hadn't heard a breath. It was so quiet. So quiet. Her last breath—it was a very easy breath. I think we were kind of meditating together and she just stopped breathing. I remember feeling relief. The last few weeks had been hard and she was ready. And she had won her battle. She had wanted to live long enough for my sister to get to keep her monthly Social Security check. And she did. It was March 1.

"I didn't want my mom to be wisked away. I spent more time in her room, which I realized had once been my bedroom, the room I grew up in. She looked so beautiful and so at peace. The room was filled with sunlight. I kept on taking pictures in my mind of my mom and the event that had just happened. But after a while, even the hospice people didn't like the idea of her being there too long. So they finally called the funeral parlor. But the funeral director went to the hospice in Lapeer, thinking that's where my mother was. He had gotten the message wrong.

"I had kind of felt like my mom didn't want to go right away. She wanted to be where she was. I felt like first she had willed her death on the first of March so my sister could keep her Social Security check, and then she sent the funeral man to the wrong place. I had to chuckle about that.

"When they finally came, I showed them where my mom was. I went in while they put her on the cart. It was difficult, but I wanted to deal with all of this. This was part of my mom's passing, and thought it was better to be connected with it. I was surprised that I could do something like that. I kept thinking, maybe I wasn't having the feeling I was supposed to be having. I felt so calm and in control, not at all nervous and upset. But later on I was really glad I had been so involved."

Resources

Here is a list of books, video- and audio tapes, and organizations that may inform, educate, and inspire you.

Books

General Reading

Patricia Anderson (1991) *Affairs in Order: A Complete Resource Guide to Death and Dying.* New York: Macmillan Publications.

Ernest Becker (1973) *The Denial of Death.* New York: Macmillan, Free Press.

Francesca Fremantle and Chogyman Trungpa, trans. (1975) *The Tibetan Book of the Dead.* Berkeley, CA: Shambhala Publications.

Earl A. Grollman (1990) *Talking About Death: A Dialogue Between Parent and Child.* 3rd ed. Boston: Beachon Press.

Philip Kapleau (1989) *The Wheel of Life and Death.* New York: Doubleday.

Elizabeth Kubler-Ross.
(1974) *Questions and Answers on Death and Dying.* New York: Macmillan, Collier Books.

(1975) *Death: The Final Stage of Growth.* Englewood Cliffs, NJ: Prentice-Hall, Spectrum Books.

(1982) *On Death and Dying.* New York: Macmillan, Collier Books.

Stephen Levine.
(1982) *Who Dies? An Investigation of Conscious Living and Dying.* New York: Doubleday.

(1984) *Meetings at the Edge: Dialogues with the Grieving and the Dying, the Healing and the Healed.* New York: Doubleday, Anchor Books.

(1989) *Healing into Life and Death.* New York: Doubleday, Anchor Press.

Lewis Thomas (1975) *The Lives of a Cell: Notes of a Biology Watcher.* New York: Bantam Books.

William Wharton (1981) *Dad.* New York: Avon Books.

To Help with Grieving

Edward Myers (1987) *When Parents Die: A Guide for Adults.* New York: Penguin Books.

The Funeral, Burial

Lisa Carlson (1987) *Caring for Your Own Dead.* Henesburg, VT: Upper Access Publishers.

Ernest Morgan (1988) *Dealing Creatively with Death: A Manual of Death Education and Simple Burial.* 11th ed., revised and expanded. Edited by Jennifer Morgan. Burnsville, NC: Celo Press.

Making Medical Decisions

Thomas Scully, M.D., and Celia Scully (1989) *Making Medical Decisions: How To Make Difficult Medical and Ethical Choices for Yourself and Your Family.* New York: Simon and Schuster,

Fireside Books. (Includes a section on how to find a nursing home.)

Anatomical Gifts
Medic Alert Foundation
P.O. Box 1009
Turlock, CA 95381-1009

The Living Bank
P.O. Box 6725
Houston, TX 77265

Legal Information
Denis Clifford (1990) *The Power of Attorney Book*. 3rd ed. Berkeley, CA: Nolo Press.

Dying at Home
Deborah Duda (1987) *Coming Home: A Guide to Dying at Home with Dignity*. New York: Aurora Press.

For Children
Helen Coutant (1974) *The First Snow*. New York: Knopf.

Sara Bonnet Stein (1974) *About Dying*. New York: Walker.

Jane Thomas (1988) *Saying Good-bye to Grandma*. New York: Clarion Books/Ticknor & Fields.

Susan Varley (1984) *Badger's Parting Gift*. New York: Lothrop, Lee, and Shepard.

Judith Viorst (1971) *The Tenth Good Thing about Barney*. New York: Atheneum.

Alice Walker (1967) *To Hell with Dying*. New York: Harcourt Brace Jovanovich.

Wellness

Jeff Kane, M.D. (1991) *Be Sick Well: A Healthy Approach to Chronic Illness*. Oakland, CA: New Harbinger Publications.

O. Carl Simonton, M.D., and Stephanie Mathews Simonton (1978) *Getting Well Again*. J.P. Tarcher.

Agencies that Can Help

National Hospice Organization
1901 North Moore Street
Suite 901
Arlington, VA 22209
(703) 243-5900

Hospice Association of America
519 C Street, NE
Washington, D.C. 20002
(202) 547-7424

AARP (American Association of Retired Persons)
1909 K Street, NW
Washington, D.C. 20049
(202) 872-4700

Family Services America
11700 West Lake Park Drive
Park Place, Milwaukee, WI 53224
(414) 339-2111

National Association of Area Agencies on Aging
600 Maryland Ave. SW
Suite 208
Washington, D.C. 20024

(Your local area Agency on Aging should be in your phone directory.)

Cancer Data Banks

For the most up-to-date information, patients should contact the American Cancer Society and the National Cancer Institute.

American Cancer Society
National Office
1599 Clifton Rd. N.E.
Atlanta, Georgia 30329
(404) 320-3333

Social Security

You will be able to find the local or toll-free telephone number for Social Security listed under Department of Health and Human Services in the U.S. Government Agencies and Offices section of the telephone book.

Cassette Recordings and Videos

Hanuman Foundation Tape Library
524 San Anselmo Avenue
#203
San Anselmo, CA 94960
1-800-248-1008 (for tape library orders)

Recommended audio tapes include:
On Death, Dying, Illness, and Grief (Ram Dass)
Death Is Not an Outrage (Ram Dass)
Living/Dying (Stephen Levine)

Recommended videotapes include:
A series of eight videotapes, *How Then Shall We Live?*, originally developed as a television series for PBS, featuring Ram Dass and Stephen Levine. (Used around the country in Conscious Living/Conscious Dying workshops.)

Other New Harbinger Self-Help Titles

I Can't Get Over It, A Handbook for Trauma Survivors, $12.95
Concerned Intervention, When Your Loved One Won't Quit Alcohol or Drugs, $11.95
Redefining Mr. Right, $11.95
Dying of Embarrassment: Help for Social Anxiety and Social Phobia, $11.95
The Depression Workbook: Living With Depression and Manic Depression, $13.95
Risk-Taking for Personal Growth: A Step-by-Step Workbook, $11.95
The Marriage Bed: Renewing Love, Friendship, Trust, and Romance, $11.95
Focal Group Psychotherapy: For Mental Health Professionals, $44.95
Hot Water Therapy: Save Your Back, Neck & Shoulders in 10 Minutes a Day $11.95
Older & Wiser: A Workbook for Coping With Aging, $12.95
Prisoners of Belief: Exposing & Changing Beliefs that Control Your Life, $10.95
Be Sick Well: A Healthy Approach to Chronic Illness, $11.95
Men & Grief: A Guide for Men Surviving the Death of a Loved One., $11.95
When the Bough Breaks: A Guide for Parents of Sexually Abused Childern, $11.95
Love Addiction: A Guide to Emotional Independence, $11.95
When Once Is Not Enough: Help for Obsessive Compulsives, $11.95
The New Three Minute Meditator, $9.95
Getting to Sleep, $10.95
The Relaxation & Stress Reduction Workbook, 3rd Edition, $13.95
Leader's Guide to the Relaxation & Stress Reduction Workbook, $19.95
Beyond Grief: A Guide for Recovering from the Death of a Loved One, $10.95
Thoughts & Feelings: The Art of Cognitive Stress Intervention, $13.95
Messages: The Communication Skills Book, $12.95
The Divorce Book, $11.95
Hypnosis for Change: A Manual of Proven Techniques, 2nd Edition, $12.95
The Deadly Diet: Recovering from Anorexia & Bulimia, $11.95
Chronic Pain Control Workbook, $13.95
Rekindling Desire: Bringing Your Sexual Relationship Back to Life, $12.95
Life Without Fear: Anxiety and Its Cure, $10.95
Visualization for Change, $12.95
Guideposts to Meaning: Discovering What Really Matters, $11.95
Videotape: Clinical Hypnosis for Stress & Anxiety Reduction, $24.95
Starting Out Right: Essential Parenting Skills for Your Child's First Seven Years, $12.95
Big Kids: A Parent's Guide to Weight Control for Children, $11.95
My Parent's Keeper: Adult Children of the Emotionally Disturbed, $11.95
When Anger Hurts, $12.95
Free of the Shadows: Recovering from Sexual Violence, $12.95
Resolving Conflict With Others and Within Yourself, $12.95
Lifetime Weight Control, $11.95
The Anxiety & Phobia Workbook, $13.95
Love and Renewal: A Couple's Guide to Commitment, $12.95
The Habit Control Workbook, $12.95

Call **toll free, 1-800-748-6273**, to order books. Have your Visa or Mastercard number ready.

Or send a check for the titles you want to New Harbinger Publications, 5674 Shattuck Avenue, Oakland, CA 94609. Include $2.00 for the first book and 50¢ for each additional book, to cover shipping and handling. (California residents please include appropriate sales tax.) Allow four to six weeks for delivery.

Prices subject to change without notice.